Major-General John Frost, C.B., D.S.O., M.C., commanded the detachments of the Iraq Levis before the Second World War. In 1940 he volunteered to become one of the first parachutists, and served with the 2nd Battalion the Parachute Regiment throughout the war, commanding the battalion from October 1942 onwards. He led the Battalion in Tunisia, France and Sicily. In September 1944 he dropped with 2 Para on Arnhem and fought the action so vividly described in his previous book A DROP TOO MANY; there he led the famous defence of the road bridge for three days and four nights against overwhelming odds. The Battalion was all but destroyed in the process, and Frost himself was wounded and captured. After the War he continued his military career until his retirement in 1968.

2 Para Falklands
The Battalion at War

MAJOR-GENERAL JOHN FROST

SPHERE BOOKS LIMITED
London and Sydney

First published in Great Britain by
Buchan & Enright, Publishers, Limited 1983
Copyright © 1983 by Major-General J. D. Frost
Published by Sphere Books Ltd 1984
30-32 Gray's Inn Road,
London WC1X 8JL

TRADE
MARK

Printed and bound in Great Britain by
Cox & Wyman Ltd, Reading

Contents

FOREWORD   11

CHAPTER 1   *Voyage South*   13

CHAPTER 2   *The Move Ashore*   24

CHAPTER 3   *Preparing For Action*   39

CHAPTER 4   *Darwin and Goose Green*   59

CHAPTER 5   *Victory—and After*   96

CHAPTER 6   *Fitzroy and Bluff Cove*   101

CHAPTER 7   *Wireless Ridge and Stanley*   127

CHAPTER 8   *The End Of It All*   154

CONCLUSION   157

APPENDIX I   *Roll of Honour*   164

APPENDIX II   *Citation—The Victoria Cross*   165

APPENDIX III   *Honours and Awards*   167

APPENDIX IV   *Major Keeble's Ultimatum*   170

APPENDIX V   *The Brigade Log—Goose Green*   172

APPENDIX VI   *Message to 2 Para from the CGS*   178

GLOSSARY   180

INDEX   186

Illustrations

Leaving Aldershot (*Cassidy and Leigh*)
Setting out (*Cassidy and Leigh*)
Helicopter drill on board
Weapon training on *Norland*
Practice with landing-craft
Broadsword comes alongside with landing orders
Anti-aircraft watch on *Norland*
Daybreak after the landings
Dug-in on Sussex Mountain
A moment's relaxation
Helicopter re-supply, Sussex Mountain
2 Para moves off at dusk
Camilla Creek House
The captured Landrover
The 'O' Group at Camilla Creek House
Interrogating POWs during the advance to Darwin
Darwin settlement
Darwin Hill—the reverse slope during a lull
Battalion HQ in the gorse gulley during the battle
Darwin Hill—the gorse gulley
The RAP during the battle
Helicopters delivering ammunition to Darwin Hill
Argentine position behind the gorse-line
Battalion HQ and RAP after the battle
Wounded Argentine POWs
Prisoners disarmed and made to lie face down

Illustrations

The view to Goose Green from the gorse-line
Argentine soldier in Goose Green (*Cassidy and Leigh*)
POWs after the surrender
Argentine Oerlikon on the airfield
Damaged Pucara on Goose Green airfield
The memorial to 2 Para Group on Darwin Hill
A Chinook brings the bergens to Bluff Cove
C Company at Bluff Cove
By Ron Binney's house at Fitzroy
Boarding the LCU at Bluff Cove
A Company in the wool-shed at Fitzroy
Bluff Cove before the air-raid
Sir Galahad burning
The march from Mount Kent
Arriving at Furze Bush Pass
Wireless Ridge—the north spur
Wireless Ridge—the main ridge
Moody Brook barracks and the road to Stanley
Wireless Ridge—recovery of the dead
Captured Argentine 155-mm gun
The approach to Stanley
Argentine POWs on Stanley airfield
Christ Church Cathedral, Port Stanley
Waiting to fly back to Goose Green for the service
Padre David Cooper
Captain Chris Dent and Robert Fox
Captain Alan Coulson, the IO
The RSM at Goose Green
Major Philip Neame, OC D Company
Major John Crosland, OC B Company
Captain Steve Hughes, the RMO
Lieutenant-Colonel Chaundler with Major Keeble, the Adjutant,
    and the RSM
Captain David Wood, killed in action
Captain Chris Dent, killed in action (*Cassidy and Leigh*)
Lieutenant Jim Barry, killed under a white flag (*Cassidy and Leigh*)
Lieutenant-Colonel 'H' Jones, killed in action (*Cassidy and Leigh*)
Major-General Frost with Lieutenant-Colonel Jones (*Cassidy and Leigh*)

Illustrations

With the exception of those indicated, the illustrations in this book were provided by the officers and men of 2 Para. I am especially grateful to Major Roger Miller, Padre David Cooper, Captain David Benest, and Captain C. S. Connor for their help in providing photographs.

Maps

drawn by Neil Hyslop

The landings at San Carlos, 21 May 21
The move-up for the attack, 26–27 May 41
Darwin and Goose Green, 28–29 May 68
The campaign in the Falkland Islands, 21 May–14 June 1982 115
Fitzroy, Bluff Cove, and the move towards Stanley,
3–11 June 128
Wireless Ridge and Port Stanley, 12–14 June 144

Foreword

This is a remarkable story in that it starts with a success. In most of our history as a nation our campaigns have started with disasters, unless of course the opposition was not up to much. I suppose it is true to say that the Argentine Army in the Falklands was not in the same league as the German 1st Parachute Division or the 2nd SS Panzer Corps, but many of their units fought stubbornly, and when we consider the weather conditions prevailing and the terrain over which our heavily laden men had to operate, we must give great credit to those who succeeded so very convincingly.

When you try to find out exactly what happened in a battle, or part of a battle, you will discover that only seldom do any two versions agree, and that in the end the writer must decide on what he thinks is most likely to have happened. This account is of one battalion only; deliberately, for this is the purpose of the book. But in studying the whole campaign in the Falkland Islands one cannot help being struck with the performances of all the other units who fought, and in particular of all those elements of the Army and the other two services who provided the essential support. The logistic problems were formidable, and our admiration for the sense of purpose shown from the very top all the way down the chain of command should be unbounded.

The media has come in for a fairly heavy share of criticism, but it was the reporters' job to keep the nation informed, and this I think they did. They will never be able to satisfy everybody; no one can deny, however, the guts and devotion of the reporters who went to war with the soldiers, and who suffered all the dangers, privations and discomforts in order to bring home the news. The two reporters who accompanied the battalion at Goose Green will ever be remembered, and their presence was a most welcome bonus.

Apart from the skills and gallantry of all ranks of 2 Para, I think one cannot help being delighted at the ability of the three commanding officers concerned. I hope that I have described their actions sufficiently for readers to be able to draw their own conclusions, and thus to agree with me that it is a great thing to know that the Regiment can nominate such men to command such men.

I had been the first adjutant of the 2nd Battalion, The Parachute Regiment, when it formed in 1941, and had subsequently commanded it through most of the war and, later, in Palestine. Succeeding COs have invited me to visit the battalion from time to time. There is a flourishing old comrades association, the Para 2 Club, which tries to keep closely in touch with the present-day battalion, and when 2 Para returned from the Falklands I had the honour of being asked to visit them again. I was entranced by the accounts of their campaign and, after some discussion, was asked to write about it by Lieutenant-Colonel David Chaundler, the CO. After I had made a very tentative start, I discovered that Captain David Benest, the battalion's Signals Officer during the campaign, had already written a very full account, having been able to discuss all aspects with nearly everyone concerned, and most generously he lent it to me.

Unfortunately whilst I was writing the book, the battalion was far away in Belize, and for various reasons, although I was able to show the earlier chapters to most of the ex-company commanders, I could not show it to the commanding officer until it was printed. The opinions and conclusions are entirely mine. The book was never meant to be an official account, but a tribute to those members of the Regiment who went to the Falklands.

CHAPTER 1

Voyage South

During April 1982, the 2nd Battalion, The Parachute Regiment was stationed at Bruneval Barracks in Aldershot, having recently returned from several weeks training in Kenya, and, before that, having completed a two-year tour in Northern Ireland. Since the end of the Second World War, the battalion has been to Ireland several times, and has been on active service in many other places. Aldershot has been the Regimental Centre since the end of the war; the headquarters are there, and most of the families have their quarters in the area.

The battalion was now preparing to go to Belize, off the Caribbean, an assignment considered to be neither very pleasant nor rewarding, and where the main task would be to assist the local government and discourage encroachments from Guatemala. The advance party and most of the heavy baggage had already left for Belize when the Falklands crisis blew up.

Ever since the Falkland Islands had been occupied and colonised by Britain in the eighteenth century, Argentina had disputed our right of possession. Latterly there had been high-powered discussions at the United Nations which had ended, as so often before, in an impasse; suddenly, on 2 April, Argentine troops had attacked and occupied the islands, as well as the neighbouring island of South Georgia, also British.

On the next day the United Nations Security Council ordered the Argentines to withdraw their forces, but it soon became obvious that they had no intention of so doing. Neither they, nor the rest of the world, thought that Britain would be able to do much about the invasion. It was well known that, after the Suez débâcle in 1956, Britain had decided to tailor her forces to a NATO strategy, and that all our effort would be designed to counter aggression from the Warsaw Pact countries. Adventurous sorties in other causes were to be a thing of the past, and so it was not altogether expected, even in Britain, when the British Prime Minister, Mrs Margaret Thatcher, ordered her own ministers to assemble a Task Force without delay and to have it ready for action in the South Atlantic as soon as could be. There was some argument within the realm as to whether this course was wise, but one thing is certain—every single member of the 2nd Battalion of the Parachute Regiment was entirely in favour, and determined to get in on the act if they possibly could.

The Commanding Officer, Lieutenant-Colonel Herbert ('H') Jones, OBE, was abroad on a skiing holiday when the crisis broke. On hearing the news he immediately returned to the UK with his family to find out the form, although, as his battalion was firmly earmarked for Belize, it did not seem likely that there would be much chance of its being included in the Task Force at this stage. However, it was included. The Royal Irish Rangers, then garrisoning Belize, were told that they would have to stay until another battalion, the 3rd Battalion, Royal Anglian Regiment, could be made available to relieve them. The 2 Para advance party was recalled, and the heavy baggage, or rather whatever was carrying it, was ordered to bring it back.

The warning order came at 1330 hours on Thursday, 15 April. The battalion was to be at seventy-two hours' notice to move as from midnight. Most of the key personnel were readily available, and those on courses could be summoned at short notice. To everyone's delight Clansman, the latest army radio system, was to be issued immediately, and although there would be little time for all ranks to become familiar with it, it was so far in advance of their current equipment that its issue was a matter for rejoicing.

2 Para otherwise was equipped with weapons common to all infantry units at that time. Self-loading rifles were the basic weapon, with general purpose machine-guns (GPMGs) as the rifle section armament. The CO asked that the allotment of the latter be doubled as he felt that his men might be required to fight with less than the normal support of other arms. In this he was proved to be absolutely correct and, despite the extra

ammunition needed, the additional fire-power was a great bonus. There was a machine-gun platoon, whose weapons could be used with accuracy in the sustained fire role, and there were six 81-mm mortars and a number of Milan wire-guided anti-tank missiles, together with other short-range anti-tank weapons which could also be used against defensive works, and the usual complement of short-range carbines, pistols and grenades. As regards transport, there was virtually none. It was generally accepted that, in the absence of helicopter lift (although it was hoped that such lift would be readily available), all loads, ammunition, weapons and wounded would have to be humped.

The battalion was organised into three full strength rifle companies of about one hundred men each, and a patrol company which consisted of a Reconnaissance Platoon and a Patrol Platoon, specially trained in those two roles. This company could include the Assault Pioneer Platoon, trained in mining, demolitions and other engineer specialities. Much emphasis had been put on training a number of snipers, who were also observers able to report direct to Battalion HQ.

A great deal of attention had been given to administration in the field, and so the supply echelons, 'A' and 'B', had been carefully schooled as to their composition and location. Finally, the command set-up had been geared so as to allow the thrusting CO to make certain that he really could command from in front, without jeopardising the momentum of the battalion should he fall. His own little command group was duplicated with the second-in-command fully informed at all times, and beyond that, for good measure the main battalion HQ, with an operations officer, intelligence officer and others, was able to monitor affairs as needed.

2 Para formed part of the 5 Infantry Brigade, which had its headquarters in Aldershot. It was not a very satisfactory organisation from the point of view of a parachute battalion, for although the HQ did its best, it was not a specialist outfit and had to command a number of units other than airborne. The British Army as a whole has never been able to embrace the airborne means of going to war. There has always been a feeling against what is known as the 'Maroon Machine', and when the opportunity arose to disband the headquarters of the Regular and Territorial Army parachute brigades, it was done with barely any

protest from those who should have known better. Thus COs of parachute battalions found themselves having to battle for their needs, and sometimes their very existence, with immediate superiors who had scant knowledge of and little sympathy for a breed of warriors they felt were overvalued and not really necessary.

But 2 Para was now to be part of 3 Commando Brigade, which had already sailed from Southampton on Good Friday, 9 April. With the brigade had gone 3 Para, which had been included with the other main commando units (40, 42 and 45 Royal Marine Commandos) as it was at a prior state of readiness. They had all gone on SS *Canberra*, and 2 Para were now desperate to catch them up. Meanwhile the CO, with his Intelligence Officer and a small party, had flown on ahead to Ascension Island.

Lieutenant-Colonel Herbert Jones was probably just the right man in the right place to lead 2 Para in the Falklands. Disliking his Christian name, he always wished to be known as 'H', and he was a man who usually managed to get his own way. An old Etonian, originally from the Devon and Dorset Regiment, he had made his mark in the Parachute Regiment as a most forceful leader. He was a keen sportsman, although his real loves were skiing and sailing rather than ball games; at any rate his hobbies served to keep him very fit. And if he was inclined to be impetuous and possibly over-ready to accept an idea before it was proven, the world is perhaps too full of the over-cautious. His one great and abiding ambition was to lead 2 Para in battle and, when he did, to lead it in the path of glory. As a CO he was most generous, kindly and thoughtful, though he could be ruthless and sometimes unforgiving when he felt that the good of his battalion was involved. He did not strive to be everybody's favourite man, but he had an innate charm that enabled him to prepare and lead his men to do their duty in the highest tradition. That he did so the world now knows.

With 'H' away the second-in-command, Major Christopher Keeble, was left in charge. His parent regiment was the Royal Anglians, and before joining the battalion he had been Chief Instructor of the Anti-Tank Wing at the Support Weapons Wing of the School of Infantry. He, too, was and is an impressive officer, with prematurely white hair perhaps giving him an added air of authority. He, as much as any officer in the battalion, realised the full potential of the parachute soldier; it can sometimes take time and experience before people realise how much they have to give.

Meanwhile, the North Sea ferry-boat MV *Norland*, requisitioned from her owners, P&O, was being converted into a troopship in Hull. Welders worked day and night fitting helicopter decks, while the battalion's Quartermaster, Captain Tom Godwin, presided over a party loading all kinds of stores into its vast car decks. The ship was ideal in its new role. It was able to take 1,200 passengers and a large number of vehicles, so there was ample room for it to transport a battalion on active service. Dates were frequently changed, owing to delays caused by difficulties in fitting the flight decks, and other troubles were caused through much of the unit's equipment having to be loaded on to another ship, the requisitioned Townsend Thoresen car ferry MV *Europic*. Eventually, however, the battalion embarked at, and set sail from, Portsmouth on 26 April.

The departure of the *Norland* was typical of those of troopships in days gone by, and very similar to *Canberra*'s. Hundreds of well-wishers, friends and families, lined the dock, and the battalion band was there to play. There were television cameras and other press photographers, looking for any odd or extraordinary farewells, although there were few of these. As at the very beginning of the whole episode, there was a continuing sense of purpose, and all Britain had been agreeably surprised at the speed and efficiency with which the Task Force had been mounted. The dockyard mateys and all the other workers concerned had laboured day and night to complete their tasks, and it was with a genuine glow of pride that those who came to cheer did so, and to the echo.

Life on board soon settled down to a steady routine of training and recreation. The space available had to be carefully allotted to all those needing it, for there were other smaller units aboard, including naval and RAF elements, who had to be satisfied. It was up to the battalion, as the one major unit aboard, to see fair play and do what it could to help the others. But *Norland* was a happy ship, with co-operation the watchword, and the officers of all units were able to meet each other in the Snug Bar at the stern to discuss and plan as necessary.

The Royal Marine Liaison Officer, Captain David Constance,

who had joined the battalion at Aldershot, arranged to practise the necessary drills for disembarking from helicopters on the flight decks, or for disembarking from the rear doors into landing-craft. Later, when the ship was at Ascension Island, a full-scale practice into landing-craft was carried out, which was to prove invaluable when the time came to effect it in the dark before the actual operation.

More time could have been spent on all aspects of command and control. No matter how well a unit may be trained and equipped, no good will come of it if the orders cannot be issued from above and then disseminated. Skill with radio, the use of procedures and the need for security over the air have to become second nature. Most units quickly make themselves adept on active service because they know they will not survive otherwise, but procedures are not so easy to learn and maintain in time of peace. The normal pressures of routine administration tend to keep those involved busy with what has to be done daily, and vital operational signals traffic is rare.

The acquisition of the utmost skill at arms is an absolute necessity for all who bear them. The time and amenities aboard ship were used to the full. Targets were fixed up at the stern and aiming mark. could be dropped overboard into the sea. It is, however, the actual familiarisation with weapons that is so important, for the ability to locate and rectify faults in automatic weapons can be a matter of life and death. The aim is confidence in stripping and reassembling blindfold, and the battalion applied itself to this.

Much thought was given to the use of the support weapons for in every unit there are apt to be conflicting interests here. Individual companies often think that they want to have their own machine-gun, mortar and anti-tank weapons at their imme-diate behest, perhaps forgetting that there may be a price to pay in thus burdening themselves with a more heavily laden element which, if it is a part of the company, can limit the latter's speed across country just when that speed may be vital. The character-istics of the weapons are such that fire can be more effective when they are sited at a distance from those they are supporting. Moreover, it is often much easier to conceal an important fire unit if it is placed to the rear or the flank of a main infantry position. A particularly dangerous concept is that the actual weapons should be kept together, concentrated, so as to produce a concentrated fire effect, but this 'bunching' invites recognition from the enemy, running the risk of neutralisation, if not destruction, of all a battalion's support weapons. However much the weapons are dispersed, when properly handled, and given good communications, they can produce support for any part of a battalion when it needs it most. The distribution, siting and handling of these weapons has always been much better understood by our enemies than by most of the British Army; parachute battalions, who often by the nature of things will have to rely on their own support, ought to have very clear ideas.

One other aspect of the airborne soldier's particular problems that received much attention was the treatment and care of the wounded. Without a secure line of communication, it may often be difficult—indeed, sometimes impossible—to evacuate casualties, and unless those needing it can be given some treatment soon after being hit, they may not survive. Wounded bodies need fluid put into them as soon as possible, and where it is not possible to use a drip, an enema may do the trick. This is not perhaps something that can be practised on the unwounded in time of peace, but at least the knowledge of what should be done, and the means to do it, was given to all. In the event, considering the weather conditions that had to be borne by the wounded, the survival rate was phenomenal; the availability of helicopters for casualty evacuation also played a very large part in achieving this.

It was not difficult to keep fit on board. The PT instructors came into their own, and most of the live-long day *Norland's* decks resounded to the noise of galloping feet. Tug-of-war was often featured, and every effort was made to keep the training interesting. The importance of maintaining the hardness of the men's feet was kept firmly in mind, for there had been times in other campaigns when the wearing of plimsolls at all times instead of boots had caused a softening that wreaked havoc when boots had to be worn again. Arctic clothing was issued on board, which was to prove a godsend, but the offer of an issue of arctic boots to go with it was turned down, as there would not have been time for the boots to be broken in. In the event, the Army issue DMS boots proved to be woefully inadequate at keeping out the wet, and bad feet resulting from this were perhaps the cause of more casualties than anything else in the whole campaign.

When the ship crossed the Equator, a sports day was organised by Major Philip Neame, the D Company commander, in place of the more usual crossing-the-line ceremony, which gave a lot more pleasure to everyone than the conventional celebrations would have. Neame had been in the RAF Regiment, and is an experienced mountaineer, having taken part in the Army expedition to Mount Everest. He is apt to be unconventional in many ways, possesses a fine sense of humour, and can always find the right comment for the occasion.

Major Dair Farrar-Hockley, commanding A Company, was made responsible for emergencies aboard. He is a Regular officer *par excellence* and has passed through the Staff College, having been adjutant of 2 Para before that. He is the son of General Sir Anthony Farrar-Hockley, the Colonel Commandant of the Parachute Regiment. On *Norland* he organised the routine fire-alarm and boat drills, and also defence measures against air attack, positioning oil drums to provide cover for machine-gun and Blowpipe teams. At first the Naval contingent poured scorn on these arrangements, for how were they to stop a sophisticated modern weapon like Exocet? In the event, however, the old-fashioned hail of machine-gun bullets had a considerable effect on attacking aircraft; the equally old-fashioned adage that it is better to have tried and missed than never to have tried at all was once more proven.

Major John Crosland commanded B Company. He had been with the SAS in the Oman campaign, and his experience there was shortly to prove very valuable. Major Roger Jenner owned C (Bruneval) Company, the direct descendants of the Scottish Company that had carried out the raid on the German radar station at Bruneval in 1942. The oldest and perhaps most experienced officer was OC HQ Company, Major Mike Ryan. First joining the Welsh Regiment in 1962, he had served with the Northern Rhodesian Army and then gone on contract to the Sultan of Oman's Forces, taking part in the fighting in Dhofar, whence he had gravitated to the Parachute Regiment where he had commanded companies in both the 1st and 2nd Battalions.

After a brief stop at Freetown in Sierra Leone for refuelling and cross-decking of some equipment from the *Atlantic*

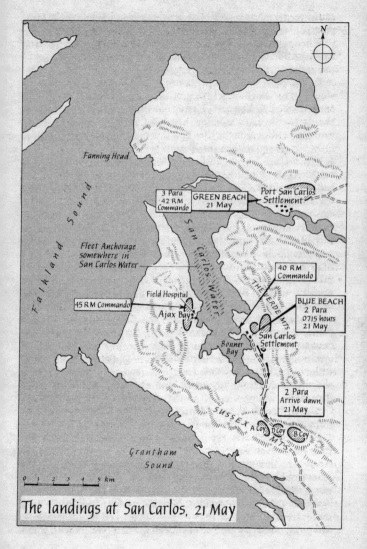

The landings at San Carlos, 21 May

Fanning Head

3 Para
·42 RM
Commando

GREEN BEACH
21 May

Port San Carlos
Settlement

Falkland Sound

San Carlos Water

Fleet Anchorage
somewhere in
San Carlos Water

THE VERDE MTS

40 RM
Commando

Field Hospital

45 RM Commando

Ajax Bay

BLUE BEACH
2 Para
0715 hours
21 May

Bonner Bay

San Carlos
Settlement

2 Para
Arrive dawn,
21 May

SUSSEX MTS

Grantham
Sound

A Coy   D Coy   B Coy

0 1 2 3 4 5 km

Conveyor, the *Norland* anchored at Ascension Island on 6 May. As has been said, there was time to carry out one disembarkation practice with the landing-craft, and early on the 7th the CO rejoined his battalion. At 2200 hours on that day *Norland* sailed to rendezvous with the Task Force.

In the meantime, much had been happening in the outside world. The previous weeks had seen a tremendous amount of international diplomatic activity, and once or twice it had seemed that a compromise solution had been reached. It all came to nothing, however, with the blank refusal of the Argentines to abandon their unwarranted and aggressive occupation of a British possession. South Georgia was retaken on 25 April, and on 30 April Britain had declared a total exclusion zone for 200 miles around the Falkland Islands. On 1 May the RAF bombed the airfield at Stanley, while at the same time raids were made on the airfield at Goose Green, with the Navy also bombarding military targets on the islands. On the 3rd, a British submarine torpedoed and sank the Argentine cruiser, *Belgrano*, which resulted in considerable loss of life among her sailors, and on 4 May a British destroyer, HMS *Sheffield*, was hit by an Exocet missile fired from a Super Etendard fighter-bomber and abandoned, burning, with the deaths of a number of her men. The war was definitely on.

As the ships drove deeper into the South Atlantic, it grew colder and the days began to draw in. At times training on the decks in bad weather could be impracticable, and thoughts of any possibility of mounting an airborne operation from somewhere in Chile soon faded. It was obviously going to be a seaborne landing in the dark and the wet, and with much discomfort and physical effort to follow.

Not that there was any depression, for the battalion was lucky to have characters like the Padre, Captain (now Major) the Rev David Cooper, who set a splendid example throughout. The Padre is a crack shot (after the campaign he went on to win the Army Championship at Bisley, and the battalion also won the team trophy at the same meeting) and, on *Norland*, when he was not looking after the men's spiritual welfare, he was ensuring that they could shoot straight. No military formation could want more from a prelate than that. Regimental Sergeant-Major Simpson, one of a long line of superb warrant officers with which the Regiment has been blessed since its formation, always has his finger on the pulse of the battalion and, with an adjutant like Captain David Wood, the Colonel knew that all his orders would be properly passed on, clearly understood, and readily obeyed. In this he was helped by the presence of Major Roger Miller, the Operations Officer. He was normally with Battalion HQ, which allowed the CO to take the Adjutant with him when he went forward.

Here then is a picture—a sketch—of a battalion going to war. A famous battalion, well trained, well led, fit and cheerful, and prepared for battle against an as-yet untried enemy. In their hearts there is an honest excitement, perhaps tinged with apprehension, at the prospect of action, the job for which they have always trained and which is the sole point and purpose of fighting soldiers. How they would fare in the coming battles the officers and men of 2 Para would shortly learn.

CHAPTER 2

The Move Ashore

The first 'O' Group for Operation 'Sutton'—the landing in the Falklands—to be held on board *Norland* took place on 12 May. This was the business for which the Task Force had sailed.

At that time it was thought that the Argentines had nine full operational battalions on the islands, together with two artillery regiments, four air defence regiments, and a number of smaller units. This force was split between East and West Falkland, but with the main emphasis placed on the defence of the capital, Port Stanley, with its airfield and port. Three other small airfields were in use, at Goose Green, Fox Bay and Pebble Island.

San Carlos Water, on the north-eastern side of Falkland Sound, had attracted the Task Force planners' interest because of its multiplicity of anchorages and beaches suitable for landing, and because of its central position relative to both main islands. An enemy ship of about 8,000 tons had been seen there recently. Nearby were the settlements of Goose Green and Darwin, situated on the isthmus connecting the two large islands that together comprise East Falkland, where there was thought to be a garrison of 1,000 men, including supporting artillery, anti-aircraft units, close-support aircraft and helicopters.

The Argentines were reckoned to be expecting invasion. They would have had time to prepare defences and to find their way about, and they would have subdued the local population and made arrangements to feed from the flocks of sheep. They were, however, thought to be short of many essential supplies, and to be poorly equipped for severe cold weather.

The Task Force was to approach the Falklands from the north-east, as though heading for Port Stanley, but it would veer westwards at the critical moment and make for Falkland Sound, where it would anchor, since it was considered that the sheltered waters of the Sound could be effectively sealed from submarine attack. 3 Commando Brigade would then land in the San Carlos area, to seize and hold a bridgehead from which offensive operations could be mounted in due course, although probably not until the arrival of 5 Infantry Brigade. Within 3 Brigade, the commandos would land first to make good the immediate beachhead, and at 0600 hours on D-day, 2 Para was to land at Bonner Bay and move up to the top of Sussex Mountain, the dominating feature of the area, although it was not known whether this was occupied. Indeed, there was practically no information about there being any enemy in the San Carlos area, but it had to be presumed that the Argentinians would patrol forwards from the Goose Green/Darwin complex.

Within the battalion, C Company was to secure a start-line at the foot of the hill (for the so-called Sussex Mountain only reaches a height of 800 feet), then A and B Companies were to move through it, with A on the right and B on the left, leaving C Company as reserve. After the two leading companies had occupied the height, C Company would move forward to an outpost line from which it could observe towards the Goose Green isthmus.

Once in position, fire trenches were to be dug and overhead cover added as soon as defence stores arrived. Initially, the battalion would only have with it what could be carried in the landing-craft, but it was hoped that defence stores and all the heavier equipment would be brought ashore and direct to the battalion position by helicopter from the ship. During the 'O' Group various light signals were arranged in order to apprise those in the landing-craft of the situation on the shore, since all movement ashore would be under radio silence.

There was considerable stress laid on the correct treatment of any prisoners. It was considered vital that the Argentine soldiers should know that they would have nothing to fear if they surrendered, especially as they would probably have been imbued with notions to the contrary. The CO went so far as to threaten to expel from the battalion anyone who erred in this respect. The dead were to be buried hastily, and in due course the bodies of British soldiers would be sent back to the UK.

The 'O' Group broke up, and the company commanders went off to study their maps in detail now that there was something concrete to work on. In particular, the photographs of the beach landing-site were exceptionally good. The only remaining uncertainty was which day would be D-day. It was assumed that at least twenty-four hours' notice would be given to allow for final preparations and rest.

Needless to say, the plan changed. On 14 May the CO hurriedly called for another 'O' Group. By now the daring SAS and SBS raids on Pebble Island had taken place, and information was coming in that the enemy's morale was low, that they lit bonfires at night to keep warm, and that they did not bother with sentries, while even their Special Forces 601 Commando Company was thought to be of poor quality. The five Pucara aircraft on Pebble Island had been successfully destroyed, but C-130 Hercules transports were still flying into Stanley. Argentine rations were now due to run out on 26-27 May!

During the 'O' Group plans for diversionary raids were disclosed: Fanning Head would be struck at 0100 hours on D-day, as would Darwin itself, and at first light air strikes would commence on Darwin. Naval Gunfire Observers were already in position on Sussex Mountain. Most important, 2 Para was now to be the first 'wave' ashore—that is, moving in a group of landing-craft to Bonner Bay, as opposed to landing in a steady shuttle in 'stream'. The battalion would land south of the jetty at Bonner Bay, whilst 40 Commando would arrive ashore ten minutes later in the area of the settlement north of the jetty.

From now on, the press was to be excluded from 'O' Groups. On reflection this sudden exclusion was a mistake: had it continued, an unnecessary barrier might have developed between the battalion and its affiliated journalists. Both Robert Fox of the BBC and David Norris of the *Daily Mail* had already fitted in well (mainly via the Snug Bar), and fortunately this order was subsequently ignored.

The final message was simple: 'Hit the enemy really hard and they will fold.' On every raid so far, the enemy had virtually run away when engaged by the SAS. This viewpoint—that the Argentines were of very poor quality—began to dominate all thinking, and it was generally accepted that any fight would be a pushover; only a few remained sceptical of this extreme optimism.

The fleet was now on radio silence. Steadily the ships ploughed on, with only the occasional light signal to break the monotony. It was a most impressive sight, with ships all around as far as one could see—this indeed was Britain about to go to war. The steady throbbing of several huge engines almost drowned the noise of the sea being pushed aside by so many hulls.

On the *Norland*, Commander Chris Esplin-Jones, in charge of the naval party aboard, noted during the afternoon of 20 May a change in course for the whole Task Force. It was not difficult to perceive that, given the present speed and direction, the Task Force was bound to go in that night. Yet still there was no indication of when D-day would occur. Everyone knew it could only be within twenty-four hours or so, and it was clear that the Prime Minister's final attempts to obtain a diplomatic solution to the crisis had met with no response.

The CO was becoming more and more agitated at the lack of information. In the end, a signal was flashed from *Norland* to the nearest ship: 'Is there anything we should know about?' The reply was, 'Yes, but it is too secret to be sent by this means or by signal. Stand by for a line.' At about 1500 hours, HMS *Broadsword* suddenly drew alongside and fired a signal on to the deck of the *Norland*. The 'O' Group was hastily reconvened. D-day was tomorrow, and loading on to the landing-craft was to begin at 0315 Zulu time (Greenwich Mean Time, rather than Falklands local time), only eight hours away.

A programme was hurriedly devised for packing away all suitcases, priming grenades, providing meals and holding a church service. It seemed that everyone else in the Task Force had known of the impending landing day a full forty-eight hours earlier. For some reason, *Norland* had not been told, although, fortunately, the delay of the news did not actually cause any major problems.

Padre David Cooper's service that evening in the Continental Bar attracted a record attendance. The location chosen had in any case a sort of captive audience, in that it was the temporary sleeping bay for many of the soldiers. Men attended for a variety of reasons: some purely out of social duty as part of any regimental occasion; others out of habit and continued faith born long before; but for most, it was in realisation of what might lie ahead, and in apprehension of the unknown.

The peculiarity of the church service in a mainly agnostic or atheistic army lies more in its social function than in any deep commitment to theological principles. Unity is found by merely being present together and in the singing of a few well-known hymns. Here was a temporary negation of the formal command structure as officers, NCOs and soldiers stood as equals—in mutual recognition of their own weaknesses, and, some of them, in slight embarrassment that they had eventually exchanged their indifference to the questions of life and death for what David Cooper accurately described as 'an insurance policy'.

Everyone rested that evening as best they could, for the change from ship's local time to Zulu time meant a further loss of four hours' sleep. The bergens were now packed to capacity with food for forty-eight hours, spare arctic clothing, spare radio batteries, ammunition, and bombs for the mortar platoon. On average, loads exceeded 100 pounds in weight.

As the night wore on, the ship's speed slowed. The fleet was now entering Falkland Sound and the danger of mines was very real. The lifeboats were lowered halfway in readiness, and the entire ship's company were ordered to lie on their bunks with life-jackets and helmets on in anticipation of an emergency.

In the battalion Command Post the radio remained on, but silent. Suddenly HMS *Intrepid*, the LPD that carried the landing-craft that would take the men ashore, called and her operations officer asked to speak to the CO. He was summoned from his cabin.

'Are you aware that in three hours' time the Brigade is due to go ashore?' he was asked. 'Has the battalion broken out its first-line scales of ammunition yet?' More importantly, 'Could the battalion make the deadline?'

Exactly how it is that such a monumental failure in communications could occur is beyond comprehension. Here was a brigade about to go ashore within a few hours, and yet it was still uncertain that one of its battalions would be prepared. The CO's short, sharp response to the questioning reassured them.

At 0200 hours on the 21st, the first landing-craft parties

assembled in the Continental Lounge, weighed down with bergens, belt order and weapons. In many respects the scene was like any battalion parachute training exercise as men crowded together, joking, talking and speculating. The many previous rehearsals now bore fruit. The system of moving everyone down through the dark car-decks to the stern doors at sea level was well known. Patiently and in good humour the battalion waited, as any slight delay occurred. It was an odd feeling. Only red lights glowed, and men occasionally stumbled over ropes and other obstacles in the dark. The Quartermaster, Tom Godwin, proudly shook hands with older soldiers as they passed.

The ship had safely anchored off Wreck Point and the ship's master gave a final message of farewell and good luck before disembarkation began. The message meant quite a lot to everyone; a high degree of mutual respect had grown between the civilian crew and 2 Para during the days at sea, and the feeling was very much that this battalion was something special—a recognition rarely afforded even to many other army units.

At sea level, however, all was not well. The landing-craft had come alongside slightly late, due to the late arrival of HMS *Intrepid*. Unknown to 2 Para, the leading craft contained the senior naval officer and this in fact began to pick up the passengers intended for the second craft, while the second craft collected those meant for the first. The result of this unnecessary confusion was that the CO had to redesignate the order of march once ashore, since B Company and Battalion Headquarters were now to land first, whereas the original plan had been for A Company to be first ashore.

The loading was also much slower than expected, the heavy packs adding to the problem as the landing-craft heaved up and down in the gentle swell. Once loaded, the first craft had to move away from the doors of the ship and circle, waiting for the remainder, while the lights and shouts of the crewmen added to the sense of insecurity. The lifeboats, lowered to the halfway position, snagged on head-ropes, creating yet more confusion in the absence of the ship's crew to assist.

Men were packed like sardines into the waiting, circling craft. There were no life-jackets, and in any case, even to have attempted to put them on in the darkness would have been nigh on impossible. The men in the craft continued to wait for one and a half hours, their only comfort the monotonous bang as one of the frigates pounded Fanning Head non-stop between 0430 and 0630 hours.

The whole scene was bizarre. For the first time in days the sky above was clear, with the Milky Way providing a spectacular curtain of white dust directly overhead. It was a balmy night, contrary to all expectations. As the boats circled in the semi-darkness, dwarfed by the towering hulk of the *Norland*, up to five satellites could be seen passing overhead in slightly different orbits, from south to north and vice versa. It would have been interesting to see what their infra-red cameras would have made of the scene below.

As men grew accustomed to their surroundings, weapons were cocked. One idiot cocked his submachine-gun. It fired, sending a round into the boot of one of the signallers, Private Day. He was the battalion's first casualty of the campaign, shot negligently by his own side—luckily the bullet only bruised his foot.

The warning code signal from the SBS had been changed two days previously. If all was clear on the tracks, a morse 'A' would be sent by torchlight—'All right'. If enemy troops were suspected of being in the vicinity, a morse 'B' would be sent—'Beware'. If the enemy was definitely in Bonner Bay, a 'C' would be sent. Eventually the craft left in a long line with all eyes turned towards the shore in search of the signal lights.

In C Company's boat an alarm bell accidently rang, doing nothing to appease the CO's anger, already fuelled by the change in plan and the lateness of the start. On the crew's radio, Colonel Jones was curt: 'David, this is a bloody shambles!'

Fortunately, albeit unknown to 2 Para, the enemy who had been in Port San Carlos had already taken to the hills by the time the first troops were heading in for the landing. No signal lights were visible from the shore, however, and apprehension remained. And mines were still a possibility; one mine hitting a landing-craft containing 200 troops without life-jackets could have been disastrous.

The boats moved into the landing formation, about 50 metres apart. The ramps at the bow were lowered and the bottom could be felt to grate on the occasional rock. In one of the leading craft the men of B Company prepared to disembark, shouldering their bergens with difficulty. Their boat stopped. Though in fact C

Company was now due ashore first, it took so long to beach their craft that B Company was first in.

'Off troops!' called the coxswain. Silence. No one moved. Again he called. A small figure scurried back along the railings to the stern—'There's still two to three feet of water.'

'I don't give a damn! They'll just have to get wet. Get off!' the coxwain shouted again. Somebody more attuned to a Para's mentality simply shouted 'Go!' They went.

Slowly, gingerly, the men of B Company made their way down the steep ramp to plunge up to their groins in the icy-cold water, the shock, as the water reached higher and higher up the thighs, finding relief in a variety of phrases. So, contrary to the press reports of the time, the first men did not 'storm' ashore at all; they waded, soaked, heavily burdened like pack mules, on to the beach at Bonner Bay. Many had already been standing for the previous two hours in waste water in the boat itself—the beginning of yet more casualties in the future as feet turned numb from the cold water.

A voice called out in English to the leading elements as they came ashore: 'Who the hell are you?' It was the SBS. John Crosland replied, '2 Para! Who are you?' 'God, we thought you were coming on the 24th!' 'Par for the night,' answered John. The SBS had no idea that the landing was due that night, which explained why no torch flashes had been received. Equally surprised, but relieved to hear that there were no enemy about, the battalion continued to pile ashore.

It was as well that the landing had been unopposed. Within an area about 200 metres square stood a complete battalion in chaos. The confusion of the change to the order of going ashore now had its effect as bodies of soldiers moved everywhere, trying to group ready for the move to Sussex Mountain. Any enemy action now would have had devastating consequences.

Gradually the companies sorted themselves out, and the tedious march to Sussex Mountain began in the dark. Silently, men slid and stumbled from tussock to tussock, then found the track again, under constant strain from their heavy loads. Companies became separated, taking different routes, only to merge again as one or the other veered from its path. C Company platoons forged ahead to secure the start-line at the base of the mountain, followed by A and B Companies. The

RSM frantically searched a column trying to locate a squeaking wheelbarrow which someone had commandeered—'Go and find that flipping thing and ditch it!' It was found and removed.

The burdens were considerable. In C Company, men had been issued rations for four days to allow them to go directly on to their OP tasks. Each patrol carried twice the normal ammunition scale, and the addition of the LMG ammunition and radio with spare batteries made every bergen a deadweight.

There could be little doubt that many men were heavily overloaded, and when dawn broke, and the long climb of Sussex Mountain began, it was again fortunate that there was no enemy resistance, because the battalion's response might not have been very effective. Some men were not up to the strain and fell out, especially in the hastily converted MT Platoon, now called the Defence Platoon: this was, perhaps, scarcely surprising. Driver mechanics can hardly be expected suddenly to develop the stamina demanded by such a march with no training at all, and five of them dropped out.

The medical section and the Padre did sterling work in regrouping casualties. Indeed, the Padre ended up moving backwards and forwards over the same route four times in order to bring all the patients into the Battalion RV, which was also to serve as the Regimental Aid Post. His whisky, issued from the dispensary there, proved a great boost to morale.

At least it was not raining. Dawn broke beautiful and clear, to find the leading element of the battalion beginning the move up on to Sussex Mountain. Although 'Mountain' is a misnomer, under the weights carried the march assumed all the attributes of an alpine ascent as men moved and stopped, moved again and stopped, each time drawing in lungfuls of clear, fresh morning air. At least the two mortar bombs everyone had had to carry had been off-loaded as each company had passed through the Battalion RV at the foot of the mountain; even so, the lighter loads did little to compensate for the steepness of the hillside.

Yet dawn, as always, brought renewed strength and morale as the sun's rays peered over the hills from the north. Mushroom-like, magically indeed, a white parachute appeared down the valley, drifting slowly to earth. This was no hallucination, but the pilot of a Pucara which had been shot down by a well positioned SAS patrol before it could make its run against the troops or the ships. Another could be seen in the distance now, weaving in circles, safe from attack. Yet another Pucara got through, followed by a Skyhawk attacking D Company.

It was immediately clear that air attack was to be the main threat, although another aircraft attempting to get through to the ships was also hit by a missile from HMS *Brilliant*. But as yet the Blowpipe detachments were not in position on the high ground, and there was no hope of getting Rapier into action for some considerable time.

Warnings of air attack became more frequent. The men of 2 Para were made aware of how exposed and naked is a body of troops out in the open when a Mirage flew over, turning and banking out of sight. It seemed to be moving slowly. No one fired. Suddenly it climbed—this was the enemy. The RSM thought the battalion should be engaging it, and a ripple of machine-gun fire attempted the first 'kill'.

Now the Army Air Corps helicopters were helping the battalion bring the heavier items up from the valley below. As day wore on, the RAP was re-sited near 'A' Echelon in a bowl between the companies where Battalion Headquarters was already situated, while back on the *Norland* the men of 'B' Echelon worked feverishly, putting stores into helicopter nets for dispatch to Sussex Moutain. The companies themselves were sited with B Company holding the higher ground to the south, D Company in the centre and A Company on the right of the line. The C Company patrols began to move forward into position.

The days that followed on Sussex Mountain were in a sense probably the most critical of the entire campaign, even though the troops now ashore were not themselves directly involved. From dawn to dusk, air attacks or warnings thereof were almost monotonously regular—all, or nearly all, aimed at the shipping in the bay below 2 Para's position.

There was something very unreal about the situation. Watching the events below as if they were taking place on a distant film set, the battalion could only stare as successive Mirage or Skyhawk attacks went in, while in the Command Post tent work had to continue regardless of feelings of vulnerability. The 2 Para position was quite unique in that most of the enemy aircraft had to pass over the battalion before getting to the ships. As the attacks went in, the line of water spouts could always be seen first, followed much later by the ominous boom of a bomb that had struck a ship. From the grandstand on Sussex Moutain, it seemed inconceivable that any aircraft could miss so many ships as they lay at anchor.

On the very first day HMSs *Ardent* and *Antrim* were hit; on the *Ardent* two 500-pound bombs had killed twenty sailors, and the frigate had sunk. A Sea Harrier had also been reported shot down, and a Gazelle pilot killed, in contravention of international law, as he sat in his dinghy after his helicopter had been shot down into the sea. But news began to come in of our own successes, with twenty enemy aircraft believed shot down.

That night *Norland* and *Canberra* put to sea; there were in any case no landing-craft available to shift 'B' Echelon stores still aboard. Rather to its surprise, the battalion learnt on that Saturday, from the BBC World Service from Buenos Aires, that 'the Argentines had surrounded' the beach-head. If this was so, then the enemy must have been using exceptionally good fieldcraft, for as far as anyone could see there was no sign of them whatsoever. As the 22nd wore on, the Command Post trailer and 'A' Echelon were established on the hillside.

Sunday 23 May saw no respite. HMS *Antelope* was hit by a 500-pound bomb that day and, despite the valiant efforts of the bomb disposal teams, the ship exploded late on Sunday night, and finally sank on the following day.

Already the combination of inactivity and frustration at the carnage being wreaked below was taking effect. It would be wrong to say that any mood of confidence abounded, and references to Gallipoli or the Crimea were frequent—not least by the CO. Still no defence stores had come ashore. Fortunately the battalion was not the prime target, for had the enemy launched either air or ground attacks against 2 Para they would have found no overhead cover, mines or wire to deter them. Above all, though, there was no clear direction given to the proceedings, and as yet no decision had been made for a break-out. The constant wind did little to boost spirits.

But already some basic lessons of defensive warfare were being re-learnt. The need for highly alert air sentries was soon obvious, for the Argentines gave little warning of their approach. Equally, firm control of our own sentries was not always evident. A visit to Battalion HQ in the darkness was not to be undertaken lightly, and on more than one occasion the Defence Platoon had not been warned of an impending arrival and had reacted accordingly.

In retrospect, it is very fortunate that lives were not lost unnecessarily due to poor passage of information. On 24 May, for example, a patrol from 4 Platoon of B Company was sent out to examine the Pucara that had crashed two days previously. Lieutenant Ernie Hocking had taken a section down the valley, and narrowly escaped being mortared by C Company, which was unaware that these troops were friendly. At the same time a mix-up of fuses back at the artillery gun-line led to an unpleasant succession of air-bursts directly over the trenches vacated by the 4 Platoon section. And to compound matters, the patrol narrowly missed being hit by a Blowpipe missile as a Skyhawk flew over!

A similar near-disaster occurred when a helicopter flight was positioned in A Company's area. The location of the flight had been passed to Battalion Headquarters the night before, but A Company had not been told. The information was again given in the Brigade sitrep together with the location of every single unit in the brigade, but among the mass of grid references, it was once more missed.

That night, Battalion HQ had been informed of the presence of an enemy patrol by a helicopter pilot who had been flying near A Company. The CO told A Company to send out a patrol in the morning to capture the Argentines. It was foggy and visibility was poor, and in these conditions the patrol very nearly shot up the 'enemy', who turned out to be the helicopter flight. The battalion had been lucky on both occasions; in 3 Para a tragically similar incident resulted in casualties.

For 2 Para, however, the major cause of casualties was the effect of cold and wet on the feet. The 'DMS' boot on issue was quite unsuitable for the conditions in the Falklands, and was responsible for many cases of 'trench foot', which put numbers of men out of action.

At this stage the functioning of the battalion Command Post left much to be desired. The CO's enthusiasm led him to want to see everything for himself, and thus he spent many long hours in forward OPs when all and sundry needed answers to problems which could only be given from the HQ, where all the information was to be had. Moreover, all the other members of the HQ needed the CO's constant direction at this early stage, so that they would be able to implement his policy in eventualities as they occurred. An HQ needs training, like every other part of a battalion, and this is something which, with all the other pressures put on the HQ, is likely to be overlooked.

Meanwhile the C Company OPs and the snipers continued their lonely vigils, forward of the main defensive positions. Generally they had little to report. Being not far forward enough to provide early warning of impending air attack, and unable to report with any accuracy upon the nearest enemy locations to the south of Darwin, the patrols were not in their proper role. The policy of delegating all long-range patrols to the SAS was a major limiting factor on the deployment of the battalion's own resources.

One important sighting did, however, give cause for alarm. Overlooking the inlet south of Sussex Mountain, Corporal McNally's patrol had noticed what appeared to be an Argentine submarine just as it was submerging. Needless to say, this news created considerable consternation with so much shipping available for attack. Fortunately no more was seen or heard of the 'sub'.

The press had made much of the appalling weather conditions that had to be borne by the soldiers on the Falklands, and here on top of Sussex Mountain the men were exposed to every wind that blew. Nevertheless, the ingenuity and fortitude of the soldiers enabled them to get some modicum of shelter and comfort, and there were periods, when the sun came out and the wind abated, when some of them felt that they were relatively well off. The RSM, for example, had found himself a perfectly designed rock cave for shelter. Likewise the Adjutant managed to find the only spot where the water table did not create an immediate pool when he dug. Generally, when water prevented men from digging down, they built up, using blocks of peat to create windproof walls.

Rapiers, radar-guided missile batteries, were now being sited in the area and A Company was ordered to provide detachments for local protection of two of their sites. Three of the Rapier generators developed faults, however, and two tracking units failed, with the result that the battalion's main anti-aircraft defence lay in its own firepower, together with that of the much overrated Blowpipe. Novel methods were introduced: on one occasion Private Worrall of the Anti-Tank Platoon very nearly scored a direct hit when he fired his Milan missile at a Skyhawk. The Machine-Gun Platoon, firing from their trenches with their normal trajectory only slightly raised, was able to produce a barrage of bullets across the top of Sussex Mountain which resulted in a claim of at least three hits.

The Defence Platoon, too, had its moment when a Skyhawk jettisoned its bombs on the far side of the bay and tried to escape by flying directly over Battalion HQ. Everyone leapt for cover, expecting cannon fire or more bombs. Robert Fox dived into the safety of the Adjutant's trench behind a boulder. Colour Sergeant Caudwell and his men, however, sitting on the rock outcrop above, blazed away and claimed another hit as fuel poured down on them from a smoking fuselage.

Similar stories were repeated often in the rifle companies. In B Company, for example, Lance-Corporal Dunbar and Private Ferguson of 4 Platoon blasted away at a Skyhawk that was following a Mirage. As the aircraft came soaring up the valley towards them, its belly was turned fully exposed to their fire, and soon a smoke trail told of their success. Indeed the Skyhawk had flown so low overhead that they could actually see their tracer hitting the fuselage.

Since the battalion had no dentist, Captain Steve Hughes, RAMC, the battalion Medical Officer, had to fulfil that role as well. His own experience in dentistry was fairly limited—based on a 40-minute film during his earlier training. Indeed, the scurry to get to a dentist back in Aldershot was mainly as a result of learning of this new appointment! Sooner or later the inevitable occurred and a soldier from D Company needed dental treatment. To Steve this was an entire novelty, and understandably he was fairly liberal with the anaesthetic. The soldier eventually began to come round, and was clearly highly grateful for the removal of one of his teeth. 'Sir . . .' he garbled, 'I've got you a present!' A grenade appeared in his hand and was duly handed over to the doctor! The man was quickly grabbed and relieved of all other dangerous dainties.

By now the *Norland* was back in San Carlos Water, having delicately navigated past the blazing hulk of HMS *Ardent*. Loads continued to be removed from the ship by helicopter, but already it was clear that items such as NAAFI stores were going to be in short supply. Fortunately the crew of the *Norland* rose to the occasion marvellously, providing generous allowances of milk, meat, cigarettes and chocolate bars, most of which eventually found their way to 'A' Echelon. Responsibility for movement of stores ashore rested with the Royal Corps of Transport Movements' Warrant Officer, a Mr Mackenzie. His assistance was invaluable.

In other respects, however, pitfalls were self-evident. Some of the Quartermaster's staff had to undertake a crash course in helicopter loading, and it was also apparent that each company required its own landing-zone marker panels, the better to ensure that the right helicopter went to the proper place.

For the Navy, the worst was yet to come. Monday 24 May has since been dubbed 'Bomb Alley Day', as the scale of air attacks intensified in two major raids. The logistics ship *Sir Galahad* was hit and abandoned; *Sir Launcelot* was left with two unexploded bombs on board; HMS *Fearless*, the Commando Brigade Headquarters, was hit by a rocket.

But there were successes against the enemy, and eight aircraft were shot down in the vicinity of the fleet. The *Norland* had had her moments. On one occasion a Skyhawk exploded off the starboard rear deck, showering the QM, Tom Godwin, the Education Officer, Mike Beaumont, and the helicopter teams with fragments. Until then, on warning of attack, the ship's company had had to muster on the car deck, in the bowels of the vessel. This soon proved quite unacceptable due to the sheer number of air-raid warnings, which meant that stores were not being moved nearly fast enough. Normally air-raid warnings came in advance of the arrival of the enemy aircraft, but on this occasion there was no warning, a Skyhawk screeching in as the cooks fired their GPMGs. For those on *Norland*'s rear deck the use of about 174 boxes of white phosphorus bombs as cover did little to ease their feelings of trepidation.

CHAPTER 3

Preparing For Action

Despite the setbacks, plans to break out of the bridgehead were now being developed. On the 24th, the CO and the Ops Officer had been summoned to Brigade Headquarters while the Intelligence Officer, Captain Alan Coulson, went to HMS *Intrepid* for the latest news.

Alan spoke to the SAS troop commander whose men had raided Darwin and Goose Green some days earlier. It seemed that they had attacked Burntside House at the north end of the isthmus, and had fired a Milan missile across the creek at the enemy. Their opinion was that the Argentine positions could be overrun easily. The SAS thought that only a company or so of infantry remained on the isthmus, and that two good companies could defeat these without difficulty. Considering the earlier assessment of enemy strength made on the *Norland*, this view and estimate was surprising.

In addition, the OPs had already reported enemy in the area of Canterra House, to the south of Sussex Mountain, and on Sunday, 23 May the CO had sent Lieutenant Jim Barry's 12 Platoon to clear the house and its surrounding area. Fortunately, Barry's presence there was now to fit in with a larger plan for 2 Para to raid Darwin and Goose Green. In any case, any move to the south would demand that Canterra be cleared, so Barry's operation was to save valuable time later on.

His platoon had been dropped off by a Sea King helicopter two kilometres from the house, but the time taken to cover the distance to the objective—four hours—well illustrates how difficult the terrain was. After using artillery fire to locate the house, Barry's men had moved in to find it clear of the enemy. The platoon had remained there over Sunday night, keeping a low profile, but it was clear that earlier reports of Argentine troop-carriers with up to sixty troops in the vicinity were false.

The plan that now emerged was for the remainder of D Company to secure the Camilla Creek House area, further to the south of Canterra House, on the evening of Monday 24 May. Subsequently other elements of the battalion would land at night to the west of Goose Green settlement, with raiding in mind. Helicopters would be used, the crews wearing passive night goggles. At a later stage an LCU would come in to Salinas Beach, north-west of Goose Green, bearing reinforcements, supporting weapons and medical elements, which would have been taken on board from the area of Port Sussex House, immediately south of the Sussex Mountain position.

Barry's platoon remained in Canterra House throughout Monday. They could see the Argentine aircraft as they approached from the south; indeed initially, as the planes passed overhead, they thought that they themselves were the intended target. One wave of five Skyhawks and two Mirages all returned in the same direction, having bombed the ships in Ajax Bay. All the pilots seemed to be using exactly the same approach route, a prominent pond being a turning point for the start of their attack. Barry suggested siting Rapier or Blowpipe here but it could not be arranged.

The CO returned from Brigade to brief Major Phil Neame, the D Company commander. The battalion plan now was to get to Camilla Creek House by first light on the following day, 25 May. A battery of guns would move in at last light. D Company would secure the gun-line and would also clear Ceritos House nearby, while A and B Companies continued on to attack Darwin. Harriers would be on call.

D Company set off two hours later as dusk fell, while A and B Companies remained at the start-line for the journey, ready to move. D Company continued southwards but, when they had travelled well over half way to Camilla Creek House, there was a change of mind at Brigade, for a prior requirement had now arisen for the helicopters to position SAS patrols far forward to

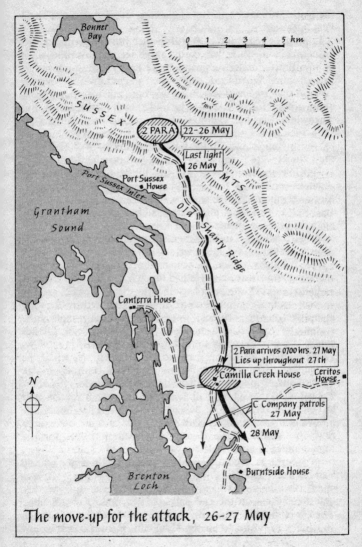

The move-up for the attack, 26-27 May

Bonner Bay

0 1 2 3 4 5 km

SUSSEX

2 PARA | 22-26 May

Last light 26 May

M T S

Port Sussex House

Port Sussex Inlet

Old Shanty Ridge

Grantham Sound

Canterra House

N

2 Para arrives 0700 hrs. 27 May
Lies up throughout 27th

Camilla Creek House

Ceritos House

C Company patrols 27 May

28 May

Brenton Loch

Burntside House

the east on Mount Kent. It was therefore decided to cancel the 2 Para operation.

It has to be remembered that Brigadier Julian Thompson, OC 3 Commando Brigade, was hardly a free agent at this time, since he was directly under command of the Task Force Commander, Rear-Admiral Woodward, who was on an aircraft-carrier not far away. A major-general was on his way out to take over command of the ground forces as soon as he could get to the Falklands, but meanwhile Brigadier Thompson had to refer daily to Admiral Sir John Fieldhouse, the C-in-C Fleet and the overall commander for the operation, back in the UK. The Ministry of Defence and the Cabinet were listening, consulting and pushing from above. Meanwhile the media were keeping the whole nation on tenterhooks with news flashes, discussions and inspired articles. Moreover, the rest of the world was showing increasing interest, and over all was the United Nations Organisation, stirring the pot. So decisions made by the Commander, 3 Marine Commando Brigade, had to be quite carefully thought out, and made subject to alteration if and when any new factors required it.

For 2 Para's CO in particular, the cancellation was both agonising and frustrating. He had little choice but to order both 12 Platoon and D Company back the way they had come, and the waiting companies on Sussex Mountain to return to their respective dug-in positions. Since he could hardly explain the reasons for this decision on the insecure radio, Colonel Jones could only give the order to return, with explanations to follow. 12 Platoon made its way back to Canterra House, while the remainder of the company turned about and began to trudge back to Sussex Mountain, a most depressing episode.

That night the CO was still determined to press for action, and he therefore arranged a helicopter lift for 1000 hours the following morning, in order that D Company could carry out a raid on Camilla Creek House. The plan now was for the remaining D Company platoons to be flown to Canterra House, from where, as a company, they would continue by foot to Camilla Creek House.

At 1000 hours D Company was ready, but the weather deteriorated and in the end only one helicopter was available. Then this too was withdrawn. There was no choice but to tell Jim Barry to return to Sussex Mountain. His platoon was now short of food, since it had left on Sunday with only twenty-four hours' worth, and the men were already suffering from bad feet, and one had a poisoned knee. They arrived back at last light on Tuesday, 25 May, exhausted.

Meanwhile the effects of the attacks on the shipping had begun to tell. The problem of catering for the survivors of the stricken *Antelope* was now acute, and the QM, Captain Godwin, was running out of time in getting the battalion stores ashore, forcing him to improvise and take advantage of every possible means for unloading. The loads, however, were stock-piled on the shore with no way of shifting them, although fortunately the local farmer lent a hand with two tractors. But the bulk of the battalion's stores remained on board *Norland* and, despite repeated requests for more LCUs, they were destined to stay afloat. It was as well. The crew of the *Antelope* was brought on board, wearing only the clothes they had been wearing when the ship was hit. Captain Godwin's team provided all 150 survivors with underwear, socks, pullovers and shirts as the *Norland* set sail for South Georgia.

Throughout the day there had been numerous air raids on the shipping and ten enemy aircraft had been destroyed in the vicinity of 'Bomb Alley'. But losses had been considerable. HMS *Coventry* had been hit and sunk; HMS *Broadsword* had also been hit. More importantly for those ashore, the *Atlantic Conveyor*, carrying additional helicopters, as well as tons of stores, had been hit by an Exocet and abandoned. The attrition seemed unending, and still, from the point of view of the land forces, there was nothing to show for it.

With hindsight, this pessimism was not entirely justified, mainly because troops ashore received very little information on the effects of the Sea Harrier interdiction sorties and the very large number of enemy aircraft being shot down daily. Nor were men generally aware that the Navy had for some time been conducting air and naval bombardments of both Port Stanley and Goose Green. The battalion sat, waiting.

The decision that a raid on Darwin and Goose Green should after all take place came at about 1400 hours on 26 May. Sudden changes are to be expected in war, and everyone in the Task Force could understand that there must be a sense of frustration on the home front, with tremendous pressure being exerted all the way down the chain of command for a break-out from the bridgehead at the earliest possible moment. The tragic loss of ships at the hands of a much underrated Argentine Air Force badly needed an answer and, although our own successes against the enemy aircraft were appreciated, there was a general feeling that something fairly concrete was required from the troops now on land.

It seemed fairly obvious to everyone that the capture of Stanley must be the main aim and that, when that fell, all the other Argentine detachments would fall. It might not, therefore, be wise to disperse any effort on outposts such as Darwin and Goose Green; instead they should be screened to prevent the enemy from doing damage, while all the main resources were applied to the chief goal, Port Stanley.

However, an early success might perhaps have an effect out of all proportion to the numbers involved, and it might be just as well to let Argentine troops have a taste of what British soldiers could administer. Moreover, the Goose Green complex did pose a threat to the San Carlos base, and while there was a strong garrison there enemy forces might be able to operate against our lines of communication between San Carlos and the route to Stanley.

Argentine communications by sea and air between Goose Green and Stanley were reasonably secure. If their troops could hold up our difficult advance through the mountains, they might be able to reinforce Goose Green and thus provide a really dangerous threat to the base at San Carlos, especially if they managed to keep their air attacks going and made their bombs more effective.

The SAS, who had carried out a night deception raid on Darwin and Goose Green on 20 May, had reported that the enemy soldiers had little stomach for a fight and that whenever they met SAS patrols they ran away, nor were they particularly staunch when in prepared positions. On the isthmus round Goose Green and Darwin, however, there was a force of about 1,000 men, supported by artillery and aircraft. They were in prepared positions, protected by minefields. They had had time to find their way around, and there was no guarantee that if their leaders were of any account they might not fight well.

Whether the aim was to raid and kill the enemy, or to defeat the enemy and hold the place, it was going to be a formidable task for one battalion, which would have had an arduous approach march across difficult country when heavily laden, despite the light loading scales. There were no vehicles, and only a very limited helicopter lift available. Nevertheless, 2 Para was 'raring to go', and Brigadier Thompson knew that there would be no peace for him with Lieutenant-Colonel 'H' Jones straining at the leash. For although it is always a mistake to underestimate an enemy, there was reason to believe that the Argentines' hearts were not really in the business—if 2 Para had no doubts about the outcome, it ill behove anyone else to be too fearful. Indeed, all those responsible for despatching the battalion, from Brigade all the way up to the Cabinet, were to be far more worried than the splendid men who set forth.

The CO returned from Brigade and immediately prepared to brief the company commanders as they closed in from their positions. At the time Major Hugh Jenner, OC Support Company, was in fact in San Carlos conducting a recce for a battalion rest centre in the sheep sheds. He was hastily recalled and told: 'We're moving in one hour's time, Hugh—we're all going. Support Company will move separately. This time we're taking everybody.'

The CO briefed Philip Neame before the main 'O' Groups, so that, as his company was to lead, he could start as quickly as possible in advance of the battalion, to clear the route and secure Camilla Creek House. Later his D Company would join in the main battalion assault. 'Once we've got there, I don't know whether we will stay there or not,' said 'H'. 'That will depend on Brigade.' The aim now was to capture the settlement, as well as to attack the enemy.

The plan was to move the main body to Camilla Creek House at last light, and the companies began to prepare their equipment. The battalion was to travel as lightly laden as possible, carrying ammunition, two water bottles and food for forty-eight hours per man, weapons and the minimal number of radios. 2-inch mortars would not be taken, as HMS *Arrow* would be on hand—starshell from her guns would provide illumination. Some companies even left their entrenching tools, in keeping with the overall policy of travelling as lightly as possible.

The CO discussed fire support with Major Tony Rice, RA, the

Battery Commander. Initially he intended to rely on the three 105-mm light guns of 8 Commando Battery, from 29th Commando Regiment, Royal Artillery, which was all he had been allocated. These would be flown on to Camilla Creek House at first light on the 27 May. The battalion's 81-mm mortars would be left behind. Major Rice urged the CO to change his mind on this point, and 'H' then agreed to take two mortars. The problem was the ammunition: as there were no vehicles to carry it, the weapons' fire effect would be minimal, since the mortar bombs would have to be carried forward by the men.

In addition, three Milan firing-posts and seventeen missiles would be taken, and the Machine-Gun Platoon was ordered to take six guns in the light role.

C Company was still partially deployed on 21 May, and so Lieutenant Colin Connor's Recce Platoon and Captain Paul Farrar's Patrol Platoon were ordered to meet the battalion at Camilla Creek House itself. Having already been out on an ambush patrol since Wednesday, these platoons were in need of rest. The long haul across country that night to meet up with the battalion did little to improve the state of men's feet, and they were also now short of food and had no helmets with them.

Back at the Field Hospital in Ajax Bay, Captain Rory Wagon, RAMC, a former Medical Officer in 2 Para, was given two hours' notice to move with the battalion as a second MO. Ten minutes later this notice was reduced to fifteen minutes! He hastily packed what supplies he thought to be most needed and rushed out to a waiting helicopter, which took him up to Sussex Mountain, where he met Steve Hughes's RAP. The battalion began to move, 2nd Lieutenant Wallis of A Company leading the main body while D Company went ahead to secure Camilla Creek House.

The route lay almost due south until the track to Camilla Creek House was reached, and then continued along the track. The weather was fine and the sun setting on the moving figures inspired a mood of adventure, and, perhaps, of reflection.

'Take a good long look at that sky: it might be your last chance.' The Adjutant's sardonic humour seldom varied.

The leading platoon had set off well spaced, in open formation, but gradually, as night closed in, so did they, until told to move along the track. The darkness inevitably led to occasional confusion as the battalion concertinaed its way south, sometimes pounding along, sometimes stopping inexplicably for what seemed like hours. Men grew tired. Gradually the noticeable alertness of the dusky start gave way to bowed heads and aching backs. At each halt radio operators would sag thankfully to the ground, sitting back to ease the strain on the shoulders. Men began to doze at halts and had to be woken.

Port Sussex Inlet was passed and a long halt ensued. Somewhere it was reported that Squadron-Leader Jock Penman, the Forward Air Controller, had fallen, suffering a twisted ankle. Later he was found by Captain Ketley, who brought him along with Support Company.

The Medical Section found the move particularly arduous. Especially weighed down by their bergens full of medical supplies, they desperately tried to keep up with the battalion. Captain Hughes had spent the previous two nights without any real sleep, looking after patients on Sussex Mountain: this was now his third. He too fell, injuring his ankle. (In fact he sustained a hair-line fracture, yet, uncomplaining, he walked through the rest of the campaign with a badly swollen ankle, only allowing it to be treated when he was back on board *Norland* three weeks later.)

As the battalion moved further south there were some artillery air-bursts over to their left. It later transpired that the enemy in Goose Green was firing on Sergeant Higginson's patrol, which had been spotted earlier by an Argentine helicopter. At the time unpleasant thoughts crossed people's minds, for it seemed that the enemy knew the battalion was moving, and that perhaps lack of radio security had disclosed British intentions. The enemy artillery was well within range. Surely it was just a matter of time before it switched on to the track, dropping shells among the main body of 2 Para? Fortunately the Argentines were not so perceptive, for had they fired upon the battalion there would have been heavy casualties in the densely packed column.

Probably the worst thing about a move of this kind is the lack of any idea of how long or how far one is still expected to go. Men staggered on through the night, cold seeping up from the ground, chilling sweat and sending shivers down spines. But they were used to such moves; and, as when having an unpleasant dream, they knew that there would be an awakening, eventually.

2nd Lieutenant Waddington's platoon was in the lead of D

Company, ahead of the main body. Eventually he sighted Camilla Creek House, over two kilometres away, although he could see no sign of movement, only the dark silhouette of the buildings. Early reports had suggested that the house was used by the enemy as a forward observation post. To make sure that it was indeed deserted, Major Neame decided to test it with a few rounds of gunfire from the supporting artillery. The house had already been registered the previous day from the OP on Sussex Mountain, and Neame expected an accurate fall of shot. To everyone's surprise, the first rounds fell, inaccurately, a long way off target, hopelessly ineffective.

Neame therefore ordered Lieutenant Webster to take his platoon in. Tensed for their first engagement, the soldiers hurried forward and burst into the house. The place was empty, although it had certainly been vacated only recently: a vest drying on the warm stove and a roast leg of lamb still in the oven gave evidence of this. Webster considered that it was risky to remain in the house, for the enemy had only just left, perhaps having observed the battalion's approach using night-viewing aids. In any case the house was an obvious target, and was almost bound to be registered as an enemy DF. Major Neame deployed two platoons to cover likely Argentine approaches, and sent out guides to bring the battalion in by torchlight. The CO then arrived. 'H' decided to risk staying inside.

The whole battalion gradually closed up to the farmhouse. The Support Weapons party, which had set off separately, arrived almost simultaneously, having made very good time despite their loads. Companies gradually jammed themselves into the large farm building, the outhouses, the corrugated-iron barn and the sheds. This was indeed a risk, for enemy artillery gunfire could have caused havoc, but the gamble between being shelled and staying warm for the remainder of the night paid off as men slept as best they could. Some amazing sleeping positions were adopted. The HQ watch-keepers crammed themselves into a coal shed, with bodies huddled against the walls and layers of feet resting one upon the other in the centre of the small hut, the Adjutant's taking pride of place on top of the pile. 11 Platoon HQ squatted in the lavatory in the house, whilst another entire section of ten men managed to cram into a

2 Para leaving Aldershot (*Cassidy and Leigh*)
Setting out. The weapon is a GPMG (*Cassidy and Leigh*)

Practising helicopter drills while at sea – men of 2 Para disembarking from a Sea King

Weapon training on board *Norland*

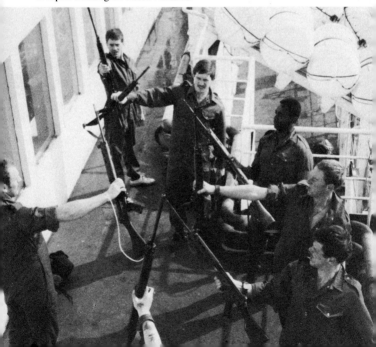

HMS *Broadsword* comes alongside *Norland* with orders for the landing. *Broadsword*, a Type 22 frigate, was damaged in an air-raid on 25 May when a bomb passed clean through her hull, fortunately without exploding

Full scale practice with landing-craft at Ascension Island

Men of 2 Para on anti-aircraft watch on *Norland*,
the day before the landings

Daybreak after the landings, 21 May 1982

Dug-in on Sussex Mountain, overlooking San Carlos Water

A moment's relaxation for one of 2 Para's soldiers on Sussex Mountain –
weapons and steel helmet are still close at hand

Helicopter resupply to 2 Para on Sussex Mountain – Major John Crosland watches the Sea King approach

opposite above: The gunline and 'A' Echelon were situated around Camilla Creek House during the battle

opposite below: Camilla Creek House – the Landrover captured by a party from C Company, together with the first Argentine prisoners

below: Moving off from Sussex Mountain, dusk, 26 May

Lieutenant-Colonel 'H' Jones' 'O' Group, 1900 hours,
27 May, at Camilla Creek House

Captain Rod Bell, RM (in beret) interrogating POWs at
Battalion Main HQ on 28 May. On the skyline are positions assaulted by
D Company during the night; on the right 2 Para's own dead

Darwin settlement

The battle for Darwin Hill – the reverse slope during a lull

Battalion HQ in the gulley during the battle, amid the burning gorse, set on fire by phosphorus grenades

Darwin Hill – the gorse gulley where A Company was pinned down. To the right of the gulley is the re-entrant where Colonel Jones made his attack and was killed

Darwin Hill – the RAP during the battle. An Argentine prisoner
helps a wounded comrade towards a helicopter evacuation point

Light helicopters delivering ammunition to the foot of
Darwin Hill after the battle

An Argentine position behind the gorse-line on Darwin Hill

Battalion HQ and the RAP, Darwin Hill

Wounded Argentine POWs helping a comrade to a Scout helicopter

After the battle for Darwin – unwounded Argentine prisoners
disarmed and made to lie face down

After the surrender – Argentine prisoners at Goose Green

opposite above: The view from the gorse-line. C Company moved down the slope towards the Schoolhouse, while D Company crossed from the right and B Company circled round behind the airfield

opposite below: Argentine soldier. The weapon is an FN self-loading rifle (*Cassidy and Leigh*)

One of the Oerlikon anti-aircraft cannon

Damaged Pucara captured on the airfield.
Note the two cannon positions on the fuselage below the cockpit
Memorial on Darwin Hill to the men of 2 Para Group

cupboard! All around Camilla Creek House, however, the companies were manning a screen for early warning of any approach.

While it was still dark, two patrols from C Company had been sent forward to the edge of Camilla Creek, from where they could overlook enemy positions on the Darwin isthmus itself. As dawn broke, Lieutenant Connor and Corporal Evans found their respective patrols to be situated on a low bare hillside, about 500 metres apart, with the Argentine defensive positions in full view on the isthmus across the water. The patrols were very exposed and it could only be a matter of time before they were spotted.

The patrols' reports were invaluable. Corporal Evans noted a recoilless gun, a type of anti-tank weapon, being dug in east of the track on the north side of Coronation Point. To the south-east he could make out a line of sixteen trenches above Darwin, with men around them digging in. At Burntside House a number of tents were visible. Directly opposite him, right across the top of the isthmus, was a company in prepared positions. Further to the south, in the area of Boca House, were a further five bunkers, and there were sounds of artillery fire from that general direction. There was another platoon position on a knoll overlooking the water of Camilla Creek, between Boca House and the enemy company opposite. Darwin and Goose Green settlements were not visible.

Back at Camilla Creek House, first light revealed that the battered house and almost derelict farm buildings lay in a hollow which hid 2 Para from the enemy's view. All the fences were down, but bits of yew hedges remained, and the area seemed to be the ideal place for the battalion to lie up for the day before attacking that night.

When, however, the BBC World Service was tuned into, the information was given loud and clear that 'a parachute battalion is poised and ready to assault Darwin and Goose Green'. The Colonel's reactions were predictable. Everyone was incredulous—whose side was the BBC on anyway? 'H' fulminated to all and sundry that he would sue the Corporation when the war was over, but he immediately ordered the battalion to disperse and find cover wherever possible, away from what must now be an obvious target for Argentine weapons. But it was not quite so easy to abandon the only real cover round about, and most of the real business of the day continued to be done from the house.

There was much conjecture as to how the Ministry of Defence and all those responsible could allow the media to jeopardise the whole operation, indeed possibly the outcome of the campaign, in this way. The soldiers knew but little of the tremendous pressure being put on the Government for action, or of the avidity with which the nation waited for news, and it is perhaps not surprising that much intelligent surmisal should have become 'father to the thought'. Anyway, all over the world eyes and ears had been waiting for news from Goose Green. Surprise being perhaps the most important principle in war, it ill behoves the authorities to put the lives of their soldiers, and the success of their operations, at such risk in this way, and one can only hope that in future a much firmer line will be taken with the press and broadcasting services.

The loss of the FAC, Jock Penman, had been most unfortunate. By the time he arrived at Camilla Creek House, his ankle was bound and he was in a dazed state, and he had lost his weapon and webbing when he fell the night before. The MO now arranged for his evacuation. Luckily the battalion's own air controller, Captain Peter Ketley, was capable of taking over and had gone forward to meet Corporal Evans's patrol above Camilla Creek.

A mix-up now occurred. No one else on duty in Battalion HQ at the time knew that Peter had gone forward. In the house, information had just been received on likely enemy positions, and Peter was then called on the radio to come in and pick up the additional information. In fact, by then he was already well forward with Corporal Evans.

As a result, just as the first Harriers were about to attack, Peter made his way back to the house. As he appeared in the upstairs room, the initial wave of Harriers was reported on its way. The Colonel was not pleased.

In fact, the lack of an FAC was irrelevant anyway. The Harriers came in and attacked. Corporal Evans watched as the fly-in began, but, strangely, the enemy did not even bother to take cover as the aircraft swooped in, although their troops were very exposed, so that the effect of cluster bombs and cannon fire should have been devastating. The first Harrier approached from the north and then banked away once the enemy position opposite Corporal Evans had been identified. A second Harrier flew in, hitting the reverse slope of the hill behind the enemy company with very little effect. On his second run in, however, Squadron-Leader Bob Iveson was less fortunate.

Afterwards he told his story to Max Hastings of the *Standard*: 'There was an enormous thump and bang, the aircraft lifted in the air and the controls started to go soft. I could see fire in my mirror and the nose had started to drop. I managed to pick it up but then the controls froze completely and I ejected at about 400 knots.' He landed south of Goose Green, and remained in hiding until the end of the battle two days later.

Peter Ketley hurried back along the track to resume his task as FAC. As he and his signaller were nearing the OP once more, a civilian Landrover drove towards them. The vehicle contained an Argentine officer and three men, and Peter's party opened fire as the Landrover stopped—each group equally astonished to see the other. One of the Argentines had been hit in the leg and the others quickly surrendered. 2 Para had taken its first prisoners, and the RMO was about to perform his first field treatment of a gunshot wound!

The prisoners were soon being interrogated by the IO, Captain Alan Coulson, via a Spanish-speaking Royal Marine interpreter, Captain Rod Bell, who had been attached to 2 Para for the operation. One of the prisoners, a Lieutenant Morralis, told them that they had been using Camilla Creek House as a patrol base and that they had been operating in the area for the last four days. This made sense, for on several occasions lights had been seen there from Sussex Mountain.

Suddenly, at about 1530 hours, the two forward patrols from C Company were fired on from the enemy position across the creek. Something had given their presence away and it was probably the returning FAC that had been noticed. Lieutenant Colin Connor asked for fire support to cover his withdrawal, but no guns were available, nor were the mortars bedded in. It would in any case have been unwise to disclose the gun positions at this stage. Anyway, Connor managed to extricate himself and his men, despite coming under heavy fire during the process. Corporal Evans and his men also managed to get back, helped by an air strike that had already been arranged. Being most anxious to keep the enemy under observation, the CO asked if it was feasible for another patrol to look from anywhere else, but by now the enemy were thoroughly alerted and any attempt at further movement in the open would have been suicidal. Perhaps one or two of the snipers in their special camouflage might have been tried, but they would have had great difficulty in getting any information back in time for it to be of any use.

At first light the battalion was joined by a liaison officer from Brigade HQ, Major Hector Gullan, an old member of the battalion, whose task was to keep Brigade informed of all developments during the forthcoming battle, thus reducing the load on Battalion HQ. He quickly blended into the team, and was later to provide a splendid running commentary on the battle.

Meanwhile the CO prepared for his 'O' Group, scheduled for 1500 hours. The battalion now had a variety of guests: the reporters Robert Fox and David Norris, who had helicoptered in from Sussex Mountain; the Recce Troop from 59 Independent Commando Squadron, Royal Engineers under Lieutenant Clive Livingstone; the Naval Gunfire Support Officer, Major Kevin Arnold, RA; Captain Rod Bell, RM, the interpreter; and Lieutenant John Thurman, a former member of the Falklands Naval Party who had an intimate knowledge of the Darwin and Goose Green areas.

The company commanders were called in for orders. Unfortunately their dispersal led to delays in getting together, and meanwhile news came over the radio of Captain Ketley's success in capturing the Argentines, and also of the withdrawal of the Recce Platoon patrols. The CO decided to postpone the Orders Group until later so as to digest any new information, and eventually another 'O' Group was called for 1900 hours.

The 27th was a very long day. After moving for most of the night, 2 Para had been able to lie up during the bulk of the daylight hours, but they were quite near to the enemy who, they had every reason to suspect, knew that they were going to attack. The British soldiers had few creature comforts with them, and all their heavier equipment and warmer clothing had been left on Sussex Mountain. Fortunately the method of feeding, which was by the issue of individual ration packs, allowed the men to feed as and when they wanted. The Hexamine cookers could produce a hot brew at very short notice, and whether men fed alone or in small groups was up to them.

The prospect of carrying out a full-scale attack against any sort of foe is never exactly conducive to peace of mind, and there must have been a fervent desire in many soldiers to know exactly what they were going to be required to do. The CO, on the other hand, would not wish to give out orders until he was quite sure that he had the latest and best possible information. But the longer he left it, the less time would be available for his subordinates to pass on the information and give their own orders to their companies and platoons. By some oversight hardly any maps were available, and without these it was difficult for officers to make any sort of preparation. Air photographs are a great help, but maps are needed for detailed figures to be transferred to hard facts on paper.

The actual giving out of orders and the stage management of an 'O' Group are possibly the most important things a CO ever does, for it is then that he has the best opportunity of ensuring that everyone knows what he wants done, and how it should be done. Ideally, he should be able to point out the objectives, the routes, the start-line and the forming-up places on the ground, but this is seldom possible, and it was not possible now.

Lieutenant-Colonel 'H' Jones's 'O' Group was a coolly and calmly conducted event, with good humour and manners prevailing. The officers sat beneath a battered yew hedge, all looking at a large-scale map. Even now there were many there without maps of their own and, although air photographs had been given to the company commanders as the day drew on, they must have wondered how they were going to pass the orders on. The 'O' Group started with a description of the ground, given by Lieutenant Thurman who had actually been over the area in the past. This is the gist of his briefing.

The Darwin and Goose Green isthmus is a low feature, about nine kilometres long and two to three kilometres wide, providing the only land link between East Falkland and Lafonia. The isthmus is dominated by a spine running NNE-SSW along its centre, and by a thick gorse-line that divides it in half from the ruined Boca House to the hilltop overlooking Darwin. A track, occasionally divided into several routes to avoid mud, links the three main areas of habitation—Burntside House in the north-east, Darwin settlement on the east coast halfway down the isthmus, and Goose Green settlement towards the south, also on the east coast.

Darwin itself consists of six houses, of which two are prominent by virtue of their size, one being the Manager's and the other empty. There were thought to be trenches amongst the outhouses. The settlement lies in a bowl, on the south-east corner of an inlet, and dominated by a hill to the west and south with a flagpole on its summit. The hill is covered in gorse, and was thought to be a likely enemy position. The footbridge linking the south and north sides of the narrow gap which closes the inlet on which Darwin sits was in disrepair. One possible approach to Darwin, Lieutenant Thurman suggested, was along the west side of the isthmus overlooking Camilla Creek as far as the gorse-line in front of the ruins of Boca House, and then along the gorse-line to the track that enters Darwin from Goose Green. A gorse-filled re-entrant running north of the gorse-line itself provided cover to the inlet at its western corner, from where Darwin could be approached along the southern edge of the inlet.

To the south Goose Green, with its population of 125, is far the larger of the two settlements, and is dominated by a large black wool-shed, a bunk-house and a long bungalow. Altogether there are fifteen individual houses, and more outhouses, and the settlement is overlooked from the easily recognisable airstrip to the north. Along the coast between Darwin and Goose Green is a schoolhouse built of wood, just to the south of a small estuary which is crossed by a bridge known as 'the school bridge'.

The IO then took over to give out the known enemy locations. As with Thurman's brief, Coulson's also took time, and in the end the company commanders were told to get together with the IO afterwards in order to tie up details. Captain Coulson began: 'Elements of the 12th Regiment are believed to be in the area, with a minimum of three companies. There are believed to be some enemy on the perimeter at Darwin, but they are now depleted. There is a minefield on the beach at Darwin and a minor guard on the settlement itself.'

Major Farrar-Hockley, the A Company commander, pressed for clarification. As far as the IO knew, there was a machine-gun overlooking the bridge at Darwin and a possible mortar position in the old corral. Coulson went on:

'One company has been moved north to stop an attack from the north following the landings at Port San Carlos. To maintain administration links with this company, the track is probably clear of mines.'

'Around the airfield are three "Triple A" anti-aircraft guns on its south side and a stores area on the north side, which may have been destroyed. There is also a helicopter roost in Goose Green settlement itself and possibly another stores area 1,500 metres south of Goose Green in a shallow valley; again it is thought that this too might have been destroyed.'

Observation by the two patrols which had been forward during the day confirmed that there was an enemy position, with two machine-guns covering the north-west approaches, on high ground at the north of the isthmus, overlooking Camilla Creek. Indeed, it was from this position that the two patrols had been engaged.

Another position to the south-west was pointed out, sited on the next piece of high ground, a knoll overlooking Camilla Creek. Over to the other side of the isthmus sixteen trenches had been seen on the north side of a re-entrant west of the inlet upon which Darwin sits; there was thought to be a platoon position there. A further dug-in position was suspected in the area of the re-entrant itself. There was a confirmed position south of Boca House, and suspected positions at Coronation Point and Burntside House.

'Minefields are thought to be in the area of Darwin and along the coast. Also mines were noted north of the school bridge and south of the Schoolhouse, but more minefields are a distinct possibility.' Much of this information had been picked up several days earlier from a captured Argentine engineer officer, who had had upon him a map showing all the dispositions. The IO concluded with information about enemy artillery: 'There may be three guns in the Boca House area. Other gun positions are confirmed to be on Coronation Point and in Goose Green itself.' In fact, as later events testified, only the last piece of this information was correct.

The CO then took over. 'In support of 2 Para will be HMS *Arrow* until 0830 hours. Harriers will be on call after first light; three guns from No 8 Battery will be in direct support, while for air defence there are two Blowpipe detachments—one from 47th

Air Defence Regiment, RA, under Sergeant-Major Smith, and the other from the Royal Marines. Armed helicopters with SS-11 missiles will also be on call from dawn.'

The battalion mission was given: 'To capture Darwin and Goose Green.'

The attack was to be in six phases: night then day, silent then noisy, with the general aim of rolling up the enemy from the north so that the troops in the settlements could be cleared by daylight, ensuring the maximum safety for the civilians cooped up in Goose Green.

In Phase 1, C Company was to recce routes forward to prepare and protect the start-lines for the leading companies, and was also to clear a suspected gun position at the bridge over the Ceritos Arroyo, at the north-east tip of Camilla Creek. In Phase 2, A and B Companies were to attack the first two positions, at Burntside House and overlooking Camilla Creek, A first and then B. In Phase 3, A and D Companies were to go for the next positions at Coronation Point and on the west coast to the south of the first enemy position, and in Phase 4 B Company was to pass through D Company to attack the Boca House position: if necessary, B Company would halt at the gorse-line and D Company would overtake. In Phase 5, A, B and D Companies would exploit up to Darwin and Goose Green, with C Company clearing the airfield. In Phase 6, Darwin and Goose Green were to be taken, with C Company moving well to the south.

Each company was to have a Mortar Fire Controller from the Mortar Platoon. A, B and D Companies were to have Forward Observation Officers from the Gunners, and each company was to have a sniper section from 59 Independent Commando Squadron recce troop under the overall command of Lieutenant Clive Livingstone. Support Company under Major Hugh Jenner was to set up a fire-support base on the western side of Camilla Creek, to include the Milan Platoon, Machine-Gun Platoon, the battalion snipers and the Naval Gunfire Forward Observation Officer.

A Company's tasks were given in detail: to capture Burntside House in Phase 2 and Coronation Point in Phase 3, to exploit to the edge of Darwin, clearing the gorse-line and re-entrant positions, in Phase 5, and to take the settlement in Phase 6.

In Phase 2 B Company was to capture the enemy position at the north end of the isthmus after A Company had captured Burntside House. Whilst A Company was taking Coronation Point in Phase 3, B Company was to be in reserve. In Phase 4, it was to attack the Boca House position, in Phase 5, it would be in reserve, and in Phase 6 also, but prepared to attack the School-house.

C Company, as mentioned, was to clear forward and protect the A and B Company start-lines, having cleared the gun position at Ceritos Arroyo. In Phases 3 and 4 it was to be in reserve, and in Phase 5 would clear the airfield, destroying the 'Triple As'. Then in Phase 6 this company was to exploit to Bodie Creek Bridge, well to the south of Goose Green, at the same time as A company attacked Darwin. To bring it up to full strength, C Company was to have added to it the Assault Pioneer Platoon, once it had played its role as ammunition carrier for the Mortar Platoon in Phases 1 and 2.

D Company was to remain in reserve as A and B Companies attacked in Phase 2. In Phase 3, it was to take the enemy platoon position south-west of B Company's Phase 2 objective, and in Phase 4 remain in reserve, ready to assist at Boca House if necessary. In Phase 5, D Company was to exploit behind C Company to Goose Green, and in Phase 6 was to take Goose Green itself.

After having supported the B and C Company attacks, the fire-support team was to move to join the battalion in Phase 4, remaining in reserve for Phases 5 and 6. The CO realised that once the D Company first objective, the second of the two positions overlooking Camilla Creek, was taken the fire-support group would have to move, since it would be out of range when the rifle companies moved on further south.

Indirect fire support consisted of HMS *Arrow*, a Type 21 frigate with a 4.5-inch gun, on priority call to C Company as the start-lines were being cleared; in Phase 2 *Arrow* was on priority call to B Company and the three 105-mm guns to A; in Phase 3 *Arrow* was to support D Company with the guns supporting A; and in Phase 4 the ship and the guns were on priority call to B Company, or D Company if it passed through at Boca House. The mortars were to remain in reserve throughout until Phases 5 and 6, when they were to be on priority call to A Company, with the guns supporting D Company and the Milan and Machine-Gun Platoons on call to B Company.

Other points of detail were tied up. The RAP and Battalion HQ were to move along the main track. C Company was to move off immediately after last light, followed by Support Company. A Company was to move at about 0300 hours, dependent upon the company commander's discretion. Ideally Phase 2 (the A and B Company attacks) was to begin at 0600 hours, Phase 3 (A Company to Coronation Point and D Company to the platoon position the west coast) at 0700 hours, Phase 4 (attack on Boca House) by 0800 hours, Phase 5 (exploitation up to Darwin and Goose Green) by 0900 hours and Phase 6 (capture of the two settlements) by 1030 hours—dawn.

As regards the Blowpipe anti-aircraft support, the Royal Artillery detachment was to remain at Camilla Creek House to protect the gun-line, while the Royal Marines detachment moved forward as the battalion did so. Forward Air Control would be the responsibility of Major Kevin Arnold, the NGFO. Ammunition re-supply was to be by use of the captured Landrover once the mortars had been brought forward, and Scout and Gazelle helicopters would be on call after first light for re-supply forward and casualty evacuation rearwards. POWs were to be collected at Battalion HQ under the arrangements of the RSM, and the CO once more reiterated his views on the taking and correct treatment of prisoners.

Major Mike Ryan, commanding HQ Company, now made all the arrangements for operating 'A' Echelon from Camilla Creek House, which was to prove a godsend to the smooth running of the battalion in action.

Thus by nightfall the plan had been given. As his orders came to an end, Lieutenant-Colonel Jones stressed a final point: 'All previous evidence suggests that if the enemy is hit hard he will crumble.'

CHAPTER 4

Darwin and Goose Green

It was dark by the time company commanders moved back from the 'O' Group to give out their orders to their platoons. No one, however, had any doubt about what they had to do. 'H' had not had many options open to him, since there was no way of outflanking or surprising the enemy. He had to try to roll them up from north to south, although it would have been much better if the battalion had been allotted more support. However, because of the pressure from above, everything was having to be done at once and instead of being allowed to concentrate on the first step at Goose Green, the Brigadier had to break out from the San Carlos bridgehead all round. So now, away to the north, 3 Para and 45 Commando were also on the move, and they too had to be supported—hence the very meagre allowance of only three artillery pieces for 2 Para.

As orders were being passed and regrouping carried out in the dark, the untoward results of the rapid move from Sussex Mountain caught up. The guns of the Machine-Gun Platoon were to have a sustained-fire role in the coming battle, but all the tripods, sights and aiming indicators were back on Sussex Mountain and had to be ferried forward by helicopter; understandably perhaps, not all the correct equipment was sent and as a result only three of the platoon's guns were complete and ready for their proper task.

The fire-support team under Major Hugh Jenner moved off at 2300 hours: the Milan Platoon, machine-guns, snipers, assault engineers as ammunition carriers, and Major Arnold, the

NGFO. He had been given the list of enemy targets by the IO and had only to await the availability of HMS *Arrow* to begin his job.

The support team moved into position on the edge of Camilla Creek by 0200 hours, and could hear Argentine voices from the defended positions across the water. At about 0230 hours Arnold began to direct HMS *Arrow*'s gunfire. In particular he was trying to use counter-battery fire on the flash of an enemy gun to the south, as well as being prepared to fire into the area of Burntside House once A Company was ready. The fire-support teams waited in the darkness, wary of giving their positions away before the attacks began. Milan was not going to be a lot of use in the dark even then, but at least it was available if the attacks slowed down in the morning.

C Company had already set off on its preliminary mission. While reconnoitring routes and securing start-lines is a man-power-consuming task, the general opinion of the beneficiaries—the rifle companies—was that it was most helpful that the problems of navigation could be left to the C Company guides, so that their own company commanders were free to deal with other matters.

The Recce Platoon had skirted the fence-lines around the east of Burntside Pond to A Company's start-line. The going was difficult and the streams, appearing so innocuous on the map, had proved to be sunken into steep-sided ravines. Having found the right place east of the house, Connor had returned to the battalion RV to pick up A Company, which left Camilla Creek House at 0220 hours.

As C Company waited, their task completed, and A and B companies began their moves forward, a strange sound broke the silence, as though hundreds of men were running very fast towards Company HQ. Fears of a sudden Argentine attack rose, and everyone prepared for the onslaught. But it turned out to be a herd of horses galloping by, and a sigh of relief was raised all round.

The approach march for the two attacking companies was difficult and, because of ravines, A Company occasionally was forced to move in single file. Finally, at 0635 hours, the company prepared to attack Burntside House, with 2nd Lieutenant Mark Coe's 2 Platoon on the right, 2nd Lieutenant Guy Wallis's 3

Platoon on the left and Sergeant Barrett's 1 Platoon in reserve—the latter's own officer, Lieutenant John Shaw, had unfortunately injured his knee on the way to Camilla Creek House, and had stayed there.

Command and control were difficult in the darkness and even finding the house was a problem. The registration of the naval gunfire on to the house had begun at 0545 hours, and because this took some time the company was slightly late. The bursting shells served to light the objective, but the lack of other means of illumination was already being felt, and the decision to leave the 2-inch mortars on Sussex Mountain was now much regretted.

Wallis's platoon moved forward from the east to capture the house. The 84-mm Carl Gustav anti-tank rocket launcher was fired—it missed! The team reloaded and fired again. A misfire occurred. The unfired missile was carefully unloaded, and a third missile fired—again, misfire. 3 Platoon then poured fire into the house, using 66-mm rockets, machine-guns and rifles.

As they closed to within grenade range, Wallis's men heard voices in Spanish from inside. They ceased fire and replied as best they could in the same language, calling for those inside to surrender. The men who emerged were not enemy troops, however, but civilians who thought that the platoon was Argentine. Dazed and shaken, but otherwise unhurt, four civilians emerged from under a pile of mattresses where they had been sheltering. In fact the short engagement resulted in two enemy killed, found after the battle. An enemy platoon had fled as A Company attacked, and the remnants of a hastily evacuated Argentine field kitchen were found in the outhouse to the main building.

Once 3 Platoon had cleared Burntside House itself, Sergeant Barrett moved his men up to the right towards Burntside Pond, north of the house, to investigate another suspect position where camouflage nets had been noted by Corporal Evans's patrol the day before. 1 Platoon could find nothing, however. By now tracers were coming over from the B Company battle to the west. A Company reorganised, silhouetted by the flames of a burning peat stack, set alight during the engagement.

It was just past 0700 hours, with only three and a half hours to go before first light, when B Company crossed the start-line marked by C Company Patrol Platoon. The leading section,

Corporal Margerison's men, and indeed everyone in B Company had few doubts as to the scale of the enemy they were up against. The orders had been well disseminated by their company commander, Major John Crosland, and everyone knew that the enemy positions were well sited and prepared. More succinctly, Crosland had simply told his men, 'There are f——g hundreds of the b——s.'

No mines were encountered as B Company moved on to the top of the neck of the isthmus. This was a relief for, being the narrowest part, the area was an ideal site for a minefield. The Argentine defences had been laid out for opposing a seaborne assault, and it was now probably too late for them to be readjusted or re-sited. Neither was there any wire.

The company moved forward, with Lieutenant Ernie Hocking's 4 Platoon on the right, 6 Platoon under Lieutenant Clyde Chapman on the left, and Lieutenant Geoff Weighell's 5 Platoon in reserve. Fortunately complete surprise was achieved, but as 6 Platoon edged forward, with the track to Goose Green on its left, Private McKee suddenly shouted, 'Look out—scarecrow in front!' This was no scarecrow, however. The figure got up and actually moved forward through Corporal Margerison's section. Margerison could not make out what it was in the dark, and did not know whether to open fire or not, since by so doing he might give the company's position away. He challenged the moving figure. There was no reply. Again he challenged, and made signs for the man to put up his hands, but with no result—perhaps the poncho that he was wearing prevented the man from complying. Taking no more chances, Corporal Margerison fired and the figure collapsed.

Just then the corporal spotted a trench system on the left of the track and warned his platoon commander, Lieutenant Chapman, who took over, leading the section in a swift attack through the line of trenches, using grenades and white phosphorus, machine-guns and M-79 grenade-launchers as they went. The radio operator provided a running commentary to Company Head-quarters.

About nine enemy were killed. It was not possible to tell the exact number, owing to the effect of the burning white phosphorus in the dug-out. The unwillingness or inability of the enemy to defend themselves was pathetic; possibly these were administrative troops sent forward from Goose Green on a rotation basis. Most of the Argentine soldiers hid under their blankets, with their rifles propped against the side of their trenches, and in one instance a moving foot betrayed a presence.

The section was elated: the men had come through their baptism of fire successfully. The platoon had fought a well co-ordinated battle, with the commander just behind the assaulting sections, ready to bring in his reserve if needed, and pointing out defences not yet noticed by the sections. The thorough training in Aldershot had been vindicated.

The company pushed on. On the right, to its surprise, 4 Platoon met nothing, although whether the platoon was too far to the left to hit the expected enemy position or whether the enemy had gone was not certain. After 4 Platoon had swept through, 5 Platoon was directed further to the right and came across six empty trenches that showed signs of having been hastily evacuated.

5 Platoon was then ordered to push on to what was formerly D Company's Phase 3 objective. There they encountered more trenches, empty and hastily abandoned, with mortars and rocket-launchers left *in situ*, and Corporal Connor's section on the left found more abandoned trenches. 2 Section under Lance-Corporal Dance was sent to the right, and after brief contact took two prisoners. He continued his attack, taking two more trenches and another prisoner.

At this point 5 Platoon came under fire from enemy to its front and called for light. As the flares lit up the sky two trenches were identified, and Sergeant Aird went forward and fired two rounds at them from the M-79 grenade-launcher. Still the platoon was under fire. Lieutenant Weighell called for covering fire from Private Philpott in Lance-Corporal Dance's section as both he and Sergeant Aird went forward with grenades and dealt with the trench from whence the trouble came, but the sound of weapons being cocked could be heard further to the west. The whole incident had taken about half an hour, and now the prisoners were escorted to Company HQ.

By now B Company was well dispersed, and the only way for men to maintain contact with each other was by continually shouting. Eventually Major Crosland had to use mini-flares to locate all his platoons, and gradually they were able to close up and re-group—the platoons closed in from the most unexpected directions, illustrating the problems of fighting at night in difficult terrain. And there was, too, continuous noise of enemy and battalion small-arms fire, which went fair to make voice control between the sections within the platoons extremely difficult. It was only through really good team work and a determination to get at the enemy that the men were able to keep direction.

Throughout the 5 Platoon battle, life in Company Headquarters had grown quite uncomfortable. Enemy artillery and mortar fire had been incoming for some time; indeed, two rounds actually landed between the company commander and his second-in-command, but failed to explode. Similarly in 6 Platoon one shell landed only twenty metres from Corporal Margerison—'Did yer see that sod?' his gunner, Private French, enquired. Again luck was with them: 'that sod' did not explode.

During these series of skirmishes, a direct-fire support system was tried. The idea, as had been laid down in the 'O' Group, was that, instead of being dispersed in sections or individual detachments, the support machine-guns and Milans would be concentrated under the direct control of the Support Company commander, so that they could produce a really heavy weight of fire at the vital time and place. The system was being tried out for the first time in this battle, although it had not been practised before. But in this particular operation, which was virtually an advance, the weapons could only provide support during the early phase, and would have to be moved before they could be effective again, which would take time. As it was, they could only support B Company during its first attack, since the more distant objectives were out of range, and had the original timings been adhered to, these weapons would never have been able to provide support in the subsequent phases for the other companies.

D Company, in reserve during Phase 2, had set off behind Battalion Main HQ, along the main track. Despite the fact that other companies were already ahead, navigation remained a problem and an hour was lost when the company turned south at the first stream, to the south-west of Burntside House, thinking that it was at the battalion RV. The C Company guide had been missed en route, and by the time it met the CO at the RV the company had actually managed to get ahead of him. 'H' was worried about the slow progress so far, and told Major Neame to sweep on forward on both sides of the track; he, meanwhile, went on ahead of D Company with his party until they came under fire themselves.

B Company was somewhere on the right. It was a very dark night and HMS *Arrow* could contribute only a limited number of illuminating rounds, which added to the problems facing 2 Para. As D Company pushed forward along the right-hand side of the track, it was fired at from further to the right; there was an added danger here in that there might be an accidental clash between the two companies, for B and D were now very close. Within D Company, 12 Platoon was ahead with 11 Platoon behind and to its left, while 10 Platoon was on the right, behind 12.

10 Platoon took the brunt of the fire from the right, but with 12 close in front the men had to be extremely careful about returning it. The 10 Platoon commander, Lieutenant Webster, saw six weapon pits ahead and, crawling within range, dealt with the first with a phosphorus grenade. His group then came under heavy fire from short range, and Corporal Cork was hit in the stomach and Private Mort in the arm. Meanwhile, further ahead, 12 Platoon bumped into other enemy positions on a small ridge to its front. The company commander now moved 11 Platoon round to the right of these positions, whilst encouraging 12 to clear the enemy on its immediate front. 11 Platoon closed with the enemy as a result of its flanking manoeuvre, and although Lance-Corporal Bingley was killed here the positions were once again taken, mainly with the help of phosphorus grenades.

The fighting became very confused, for the company was in the midst of a defensive system, but the sections were extremely well led by their young NCOs, and dealt with the opposition effectively whenever they met them. There was no doubt that the Argentine soldiers were no match for 2 Para in the dark. Whenever there was a clash in the open, the result was the same—the enemy soldiers were either killed or taken prisoner. There were some narrow escapes, too. Private Parr was hit in the stomach, but the bullet was deflected by his belt and lodged harmlessly in his navel.

When the action was over, Neame used flares to help collect his men together. He then went through the positions again as far as possible to make sure that they really were clear. Throughout the action there had been virtually no support, for even if it had been possible to direct the fire from HMS *Arrow*, her one gun had jammed at the *moment critique*.

Realising that he could no longer be of any use from the far side of Camilla Creek, Major Hugh Jenner asked, and received, permission to move Support Company and its weapons round and join the rest of the battalion on the isthmus. His teams set off at 0850 hours. C Company, in reserve at this time, also moved forward before first light, having been joined by the Assault Pioneer Platoon, which had brought ammunition up, but which would now be needed to collect and deal with D Company's casualties. C Company was thus down to two platoons once more.

There was considerable enemy artillery activity by this time, much of it attracted to a burning peat stack near Battalion HQ, situated just behind the D Company battle. Fortunately, perhaps owing to the softness of the ground, many of the shells failed to explode, and the effects of those that did go off were much reduced. One landed slap between the CO and the Adjutant. 'Lucky that they are using such lousy ammunition,' was the comment—'H' was in his element.

Battalion HQ had been sited just behind D Company during the latter's battle. The RAP was set up, and the D Company casualties began to arrive. Corporal Cork and Private Fletcher were eventually located. Both were dead. Fletcher was found lying beside his corporal, a shell-dressing opened in his hand; he had been hit while attempting to save Cork's life.

Casualty evacuation was a slow and painful process, and was hampered by enemy artillery fire. There were no stretchers, and bodies had to be laid on ponchos and then carried in a hammock-like contraption—a very tiring business indeed.

Colonel Jones now ordered A Company to push on to Coronation Point, its Phase 3 objective. Command and control proved easier after the dress rehearsal of Burntside House, and the company was in high spirits as it moved towards Darwin. It was still only 0920 hours when they arrived at the south end of the Coronation Point feature, having found it clear of enemy.

On arrival at the northern edge of the inlet north of Darwin itself, Major Farrar-Hockley went forward to confirm his position. He then asked permission to move on in the darkness to take Darwin Hill before first light. The CO came up to satisfy himself about the situation and, on seeing the form, immediately gave the go-ahead, indeed, he urged all possible speed.

Meanwhile B Company had re-grouped and had begun to move forward again. During their passage down the isthmus they had been trying to fix their position—when asked to give his location now, John Crosland replied: '400 yards west of the moon, for all I know', a comment that perfectly summarises the difficulties. He hoped that he was heading towards the ridge that dominated Boca House.

A Company's plan was to have a fire-support platoon at the mouth of the inlet on its northern side overlooking Darwin settlement, to cover the threat from the known enemy machine-gun post and other positions, while the remainder of the company moved round the inlet and up onto the higher ground above Darwin. 2nd Lieutenant Wallis's 3 Platoon set off to take up position at the north end of the causeway to cover Darwin, while 1 and 2 Platoons made ready.

As first light approached, 2nd Lieutenant Coe's 2 Platoon led the company forward. Conscious of the danger from the high ground to his front and right, he ordered the lead section into arrowhead formation, keeping his rear sections in file. As he skirted the western edge of the inlet, he could see a steep-sided re-entrant or gully filled with gorse ahead: this was to be his route to the high ground, from where the company could sweep left into Darwin.

With his company commander urging him on, there was no time for 2nd Lieutenant Coe to deploy a section on to the spur on the right of the re-entrant to cover the platoon forward, and he himself was right up behind the leading section. Suddenly three figures appeared on a mound to the right, silhouetted against the now-lightening sky. It was thought that they might be civilians. 'Perhaps it's a man walking his dog,' someone said. Corporal Spencer was only a few yards away and noticed that the men had weapons. He called to them in English. They replied in Spanish—Argentines. They waved, perhaps thinking that the troops below were Argentine also, until realising their mistake, one put up his hands, the second ran, and the third dropped as the platoon engaged.

Corporal Camp's section was now in the gully itself, and

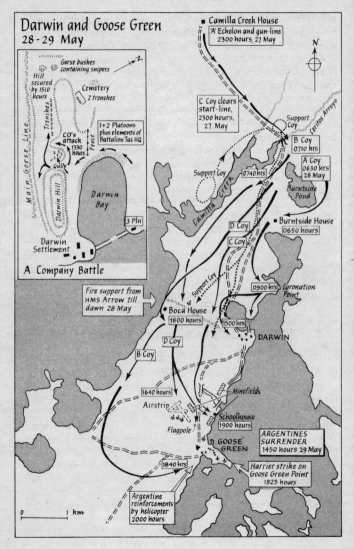

Darwin and Goose Green
28-29 May

■ Camilla Creek House

'A' Echelon and gun-line
2300 hours, 27 May

N

Gorse bushes
containing snipers

Hill
secured
by 1510
hours

Cemetery
2 trenches

C Coy clears
start-line,
2300 hours,
27 May

Support
Coy

1 + 2 Platoons
plus elements of
Battalion Tac HQ

CO's
attack
1330
hours

Fence

B Coy
0710 hrs

A Coy
0630 hrs
28 May

Gully

Support Coy

0740 hrs

Burntside
Pond

Darwin Hill

Darwin
Bay

3 Pln

D Coy

C Coy

Burntside House
0650 hours

Darwin
Settlement

A Company Battle

Support Coy

0900 hrs

Coronation
Point

Fire support from
HMS *Arrow till*
dawn 28 May

Boca House
1600 hours

1500 hrs

DARWIN

D Coy

B Coy

1640 hours

Minefields

Airstrip

Flagpole

Schoolhouse
1900 hours

GOOSE
GREEN

ARGENTINES
SURRENDER
1450 hours 29 May

1840 hrs

Harrier strike on
Goose Green Point
1925 hours

Argentine
reinforcements
by helicopter
2000 hours

0   1 km

Corporal Hardman's section followed, but Corporal Adams and the right rear section came under heavy fire from enemy trenches on the spur. Caught in the open, the corporal bravely led his men to charge forward to the other side of the spur, where another gully offered some protection, all the time thinking this to be only a small enemy position. In fact, he was just below the line of trenches identified the day before.

Corporal Adams was shot and wounded in the shoulder, and Private Tuffen, the machine-gunner, was also hit. Realising the scale of the opposition, Corporal Adams led his men back round the tip of the spur to rejoin 2 Platoon in the gorse-filled gully. For the time being Tuffen lay on the shoulder of the mound where he had been hit; to try to reach him would have been suicidal.

Sergeant Barrett's 1 Platoon was close behind 2nd Lieutenant Coe's, and both it and Company HQ were well and truly caught in the open. It was difficult to see where the fire was coming from. 1 Platoon advanced into the gulley firing from the hip, aiming in the general direction of the enemy, but suffered several men wounded, including two senior medics from the Company Aid Post, and Corporal Melia, RE, the booby-trap expert attached to the company to assist in clearing Darwin, was killed. Then they noticed a position a little above them which seemed to be causing much of the trouble. Corporal Camp and Private Dey of 2 Platoon, and the FOO, Captain Watson, dealt with the nearest bunkers using grenades and 66-mm rockets, taking a number of prisoners. One of the captured Argentines had a wound in the throat which Corporal Camp treated.

There was a lot of confused fighting at this stage, as the platoons fought their way into the gulley. It was difficult to get an exact fix on the enemy and, the better to locate them, Private Dey, a machine-gunner, got up on his knees to peer at them and then dropped backwards, as if dead. It was also found that the only way to elevate the GPMG to bring it to bear uphill was to fire it off the long-suffering Private Pain's back. When some of the enemy were seen to be running away, orders were relayed to the MFC for mortar fire, but the only rounds that arrived were much too close, and obviously came from people who were far from friendly.

Coe, on Major Farrar-Hockley's orders, now tried a left

flanking movement with his platoon. As he was standing to initiate this, someone called from behind, 'Watch out, Boss— there's a tracer only inches above your head.' The men were all becoming used to being under fire, but were not yet able to differentiate between what was really close and what was not. 2 Platoon tried to get on to a mound at the head of the gulley, in order to dominate the enemy trenches, but the move was hampered by heavy machine-gun fire from the right. Private Worrall was hit during this attempt at manoeuvre, which was now called off. The company commander now ordered Sergeant Barrett to form a fire base of GPMGs, to try and neutralise the nearest enemy trenches with this and his platoon. Private Kirkwood was hit almost immediately, and it was plain that the process would be a slow one. As it grew lighter there was no sign of the Argentines giving in, and it was obvious that more would have to be done about fire support if the company was to succeed without very heavy loss. The men in the gulley were scattered in sections or smaller groups, using little pockets in the ground for cover as they directed fire on the enemy trenches. But the platoons were under heavy fire from a well-dug-in enemy, fighting with some persistence from a dominating position, armed with equipment very similar to 2 Para's, including some heavy machine-guns, and supported by mortar fire. The Argentines also outnumbered the attacking Paras.

In the meantime Worrall had to be rescued. Corporals Prior and Abols set out to do this, leaving their weapons behind, as these would have encumbered them. As they broke cover, Prior was hit. Corporal Hardman now joined Abols in his effort, but just as they were pulling the wounded Prior into safety he was hit again and killed. A little later Worrall was brought in, but then Private Russell was hit when a grenade exploded between his platoon commander, Sergeant Hastings, and himself.

Major Farrar-Hockley had decided to group Sergeant Barrett's fire base, containing as many machine-guns as possible, on the mound which, since the capture of the nearest enemy positions, had become much less dangerous. Privates Alexander, Rees, Warden and Brookes moved up with their weapons, and all the ammunition that could be collected was thrown up to their position. Eventually six guns were grouped together, but it now transpired that the main enemy positions were further away to the right, and their neutralisation required the battalion's mortars, which would take time, since Support Company was still out of range.

Meanwhile 2nd Lieutenant Wallis's 3 Platoon, north of the causeway on the other side of the inlet, was being mortared and had suffered casualties. The men had to find what cover they could, and continue with the task of covering Darwin itself.

Main Battalion HQ had now moved up to where D Company had fought its battle in the dark. Not surprisingly, some of the enemy positions attacked by D Company had been overlooked in the darkness and WO Fenwick, the Assistant Operations Sergeant-Major at Battalion HQ, decided to take a look round, in the growing daylight. He noticed what looked like an Argentine trench completely covered over with a blanket. Having approached with care, he whipped the blanket off to find three Argentine soldiers fast asleep inside the trench.

2 Para had fought brilliantly throughout the night, but with the dawn came confidence for the enemy, and the battle now seemed to be in the balance. As it grew lighter, so the enemy shelling and mortaring increased. Once again it was noticeable how much the splinter and blast effect was reduced by the softness of the ground. A number of prisoners had been collected, and during particularly heavy stonks they vied with members of the battalion in diving into what cover was available —at one point the RSM found himself on top of one of them.

The CO and his Tac HQ were well forward, just behind A Company. He had been jubilant after Coronation Point was taken and had sent brigade a message reading: 'On schedule and approaching Darwin.' Now, however, he was having second thoughts. Farrar-Hockley had been heard calling over the wireless for artillery support, but the situation was considered too confused for his request to be accepted as yet.

In any case, shortage of ammunition for the three 105-mm guns was a problem. Back in the gun-line it seemed that the weapons were seldom out of action, and the empty shell-cases were piling up. Because of the soft ground, the trails buried themselves right up to the gun-layers' seats, while the enemy artillery also directed its attention upon the guns. Soon after dawn, two Pucaras attacked and the defending Blowpipes engaged them. HMS *Arrow* boldly overstayed her time limit for as long as she dared, in order to continue her support, but at dawn she left. Ammunition for the machine-guns and other small arms weapons with the forward companies was soon to be a headache, and whenever stretcher-bearers went forward they took loads with them—not for them, unfortunately, was there to be the solace of an empty stretcher on the outward journey. There would be no help from the Harriers either, since the bad weather prevented an air strike.

B Company's battle for Boca House began at about the same time as A Company's engagement on Darwin Hill. Lieutenant Hocking's 4 Platoon was on the right, Lieutenant Chapman's 6 Platoon on the left, and Weighell's 5 Platoon in reserve. As it grew lighter their black-hatted company commander, John Crosland (Major Crosland preferred a black knitted woollen cap to the more orthodox headgear) had urged the platoons forward down the slope towards the gorse-line in front of the ruined house. Suddenly every platoon came under fire.

In front of 4 Platoon a machine-gun was firing from the left flank, and the men immediately took cover in the folds of the convex slope. As the light improved, enemy bunkers and a machine-gun were seen to the south of Boca House, just as expected. The platoon opened up on these, but was at a disadvantage against an enemy in prepared positions, and was forced to pull back into some dead ground as Argentine sniper and machine-gun fire grew more accurate.

Similarly, 5 Platoon sought cover in a small re-entrant on the forward slope. Lieutenant Weighell could see that most of the enemy machine-gun fire on the left was actually directed eastwards towards A Company, and the lighter the morning became, the heavier the enemy fire. He therefore decided to pull back, the platoon crawling carefully up the hill, but as Private Street, the mortarman, put down smoke to cover the platoon's withdrawal, he was hit in the leg. Corporal Standish and Private Brooke went forward to give him first aid as machine-gun fire swept the exposed slope. They grabbed Street and got him back into dead ground, running four to five yards at a time between bursts of enemy fire—the mortarman was in agony from such rough handling.

Private Hall was hit in the back, and Privates Illingworth and Poole, who were close to him when he fell, took his webbing off and, having given him first aid, dragged him back into dead ground. Illingworth then remembered the webbing and weapon, and crawled forward to retrieve them. He was killed instantly by enemy fire. Sergeant Aird and the radio operator, Private Williamson, went forward to recover his body.

The B Company second-in-command, Captain John Young, was last off that slope, having fought a neat little battle. Between himself and his signaller, Private Forbes, who spotted for him, they reckoned that they had accounted for two enemy at a range of 600 yards. Captain Young, however, was hit himself and seriously wounded not long afterwards.

6 Platoon had come under fire from two machine-guns on the pyramidal hill by the gorse but, realising that A Company was in that area, Lieutenant Chapman ordered his men not to fire. He was then ordered to skirmish forward and, using fire and manoeuvre, took two of his sections up to a previously occupied bunker. The enemy had gone. He pushed on, reaching the gorse-line. As they approached, a lone enemy machine-gunner —perhaps one who had earlier vacated the trenches—opened fire, just missing the platoon commander. The machine-gunner ran off, and as he did so, the platoon came under fire from Boca House. Someone shouted, 'What the f——is the DS solution to this one?' If in doubt, have a cigarette. The men of 6 Platoon did so, in the cover provided by the gorse.

Whilst A and B Companies were stuck, C Company, still in reserve at this time, had been ordered to move up on the left of the axis of advance in the direction of the burning gorse, and D Company too had regrouped and moved forward on the right. The companies were shelled continuously and it seemed clear that an enemy OP was watching them, calling down fire as they moved. Many had narrow escapes: Captain Farrar, for instance, watched helplessly as a dud mortar bomb landed in the peat right beside him. There was, however, some cover in the lee of the ridge line over which B Company had passed earlier.

By now the C Company commander could see beneath him the A Company platoons in the gorse, and the enemy above them and to their right. His company had twelve LMGs available and he thought that it might have been possible to move them forward on to the ridge overlooking the line of trenches in order to provide fire support for an A Company assault. Such offers of help were, however, declined at this stage, and when D Company offered similar assistance it, too, was turned down by the CO—'Stay there . . . no one is to come forward,' was the reply. For a while D Company remained by a minefield on the west of the track, watching as the battalion mortars vainly tried to provide an effective antidote on to the enemy positions. Major Neame decided that he must move his men forward a little to escape the constant shelling they were suffering. The CO noticed the movement and gained the erroneous impression that D Company had ignored his earlier order not to come forward. Once more Neame was ordered to keep out of the battle.

As the soldiers waited, they noticed a straggling group of Argentines on the western side of the isthmus, obviously trying to move south-west back towards Boca House. Possibly these were stragglers from the now-overrun positions to the north, attempting to avoid being cut off. Charteris of the Recce Platoon opened up on the enemy with his LMG, but they were out of range.

D Company moved back into the relative safety of the lee of a hill. There was nothing to do but wait and brew up. During this wait, Major Neame noticed that the western shoreline seemed to offer a possibility of turning the enemy's flank, but when he made this suggestion to the CO it was turned down curtly— 'Don't tell me how to run my battle.'

While C and D Companies remained in position but out of action, the support group of Milan and machine-guns had moved up behind them. Major Hugh Jenner reported to the CO, but was told, 'I don't want anyone to come forward until we sort this thing out—it's a difficult situation.' 'H' knew that he still had a long way to go, and did not want to commit more than he had to at this comparatively early stage of the battle. The enemy positions had turned out to be very well sited and stoutly defended, and any hasty or ill-considered action on 2 Para's part now could prove very expensive, something that Colonel Jones could not afford.

In the gorse gully, however, A Company was urgently in need of help. At 1125 hours Major Farrar-Hockley had called for a Harrier strike, but the request, although passed to Brigade, was turned down due to bad weather at sea. In the daylight the enemy had a clear advantage and, despite the earlier optimistic predictions about Argentine resistance, they showed no sign of crumbling. As though underlining the absence of air support, three Pucaras flew over on their way to their main target, 'A' Echelon and the gun-lines at Camilla Creek House. At 1155 hours they swept in to attack that area with bombs and cannon, and one was shot down by the Blowpipe detachment.

Still reluctant to commit his reserves (C and D Companies), 'H' Jones now decided to go up to A Company to try to get forward without this support. Things had not been going well and the team of GPMG gunners which had previously been established on the mound had had to come back, although the seven enemy trenches on the mound itself had been neutralised. On arrival in the gorse gulley, after a hazardous journey around the edge of the inlet, the CO found 2nd Lieutenant Coe with the company commander. 'H' asked the subaltern:

'Can you get up to the gorse-line?'

'Yes, sir, but it will be pretty hairy.'

'Can you get into a position from which mortar fire can be directed on to the enemy positions?'

'Yes, but that will be really hairy.'

'Well, I want you to take the mortar officer up there with you now.'

Dair Farrar-Hockley was most unhappy about this, however. His company had tried such a manoeuvre with no good result, and after the two officers had gone a part of the way they were called back. It was now thought that perhaps a right flanking move might succeed, and while this was being arranged, the CO said to his company commander: 'Dair, you have got to take that ledge,' indicating a well-defended enemy position above them and to their right, perhaps 60 metres from where they stood. A Company had already tried this about an hour earlier, and had sustained casualties in the process, but the company commander realised that, with ammunition running low and support from elsewhere uncertain, it was vital to take the nearest enemy trenches.

Now there was quite a stir around Company HQ as Major Farrar-Hockley gathered a party and prepared to lead it up and onto the ledge. The company second-in-command, Captain Chris Dent, and the Adjutant, Captain David Wood, who had come forward with the CO's party, were both determined to get in on the act. Really the latter had no business to be in the area, but was heard to say, 'Well done, everyone. Let's remember Arnhem.' The A Company commander takes up the story:

'Responding to the Colonel's order, I led a group of perhaps fifteen or sixteen up onto the ledge. Private Dey, a machine-gunner, was in front of me, Corporal Hardman forward and, to the left, Captain Dent; the Adjutant, whose presence I was unaware of, joined this group somewhere behind me. Our position on the ledge was short-lived. I saw Chris Dent killed instantly, and was told two others had gone down. After attempting to win the fire-fight we winkled our way off the ledge and back into dead ground. The nearest enemy was only 100 metres away, and could not be breached from this point.'

Private Dey had been rather perturbed at seeing the officers so determined on business which was not really theirs; 'You will get killed if you go any further,' he warned. As he did so, Captain Dent fell dead in front of him, and the Adjutant was shot and killed very soon afterwards, as was Corporal Hardman. Caught in a storm of fire from the Argentine positions, and with casualties including two officers killed, Major Farrar-Hockley ordered his group back down off the ledge and into the comparative safety of the lee of the slope—'If you don't f——get out now, sir, you ain't getting out,' one of his men called.

Meanwhile, the Colonel had started off practically on his own, moving round the spur and into the second gully where Corporal Adams and his section had taken cover in the early moments of the battle. His determination to see for himself lured him further and further forward. Ever a man for being in front, he must have felt that the key to the success of the whole operation was in his grasp, and that it was being denied him. The company commander was still extricating himself and his men from the vain, if gallant, attack upon the ledge, when one of the officers called to him: 'It's the CO. He's gone round the corner on his own.' 2 Para's Colonel, as Major Farrar-Hockley recorded, 'seeing our predicament and the immediate need to exploit a situation . . . had made a valiant attempt to get in among these nearest trenches with a small tactical party and disrupt the enemy.' Obviously 'H' intended to take the

Argentines in the flank while they were still distracted by the attack on the ledge.

Sergeant Norman and Lance-Corporal Beresford usually accompanied the CO wherever he went, and they were not far behind him now as he made his way up the slope towards the enemy trenches. He paused in a small re-entrant right among the enemy positions, none of which seemed to have noticed him, and from there he could see one particular post which plainly had been causing a lot of trouble. He took the magazine off his Sterling to check it, then, satisfied, he set off alone for the enemy post. As he did so, Sergeant Norman noticed another position close behind his CO, which 'H' had failed to see but which had now been alerted. 'Watch your back!' he shouted, as he dived for cover, but 'H', if he heard, took no notice. The enemy machine-gun behind him fired and he fell. It was only then that the Argentine troops he was making for realised that he was there, apprised by the sound of his fall. One of the sergeants who had gone forward with 'H' sent a brief message over the wireless: 'Sunray is down.'

The battle continued as the gravely wounded colonel lay where he had fallen, but now those who had followed him closely, and those who would have done so, seemed to be spurred on to extra effort. Inspired by the CO's action, the company attacked again—up and on was the order of the day, and within fifteen minutes white flags or their equivalent appeared in the Argentine trenches.* The company commander called a warning lest the enemy be trying a ruse, but as the firing died down the Argentine soldiers began to come out. They were quickly made prisoner.

As the enemy began to surrender Sergeant Norman ran to the CO, who was very badly wounded and unconscious. There was little that could be done for him. His wounds were dressed and a saline drip was applied and he was gently carried up to a place where it would be possible for a helicopter to land. Urgent signals had been sent for a helicopter to pick up the wounded officer, and Dair Farrar-Hockley waited by his Colonel's side. Extra clothing was found, but really nothing could be done to save him, and after a few minutes Lieutenant-Colonel 'H' Jones died. The time was about 1345 hours.

* The enemy surrender was hastened by Corporal Abols, who scored a direct hit on an Argentine trench with a 66-mm rocket, one of the actions which led to his award of the DCM.

It was a dark and grey sort of day, with only occasional breaks in the low cloud, although it was not particularly cold. News of the death of their CO spread quite quickly to the other units of 2 Para, though it was by no means broadcast, but it was to be another hour before helicopters arrived to take back the wounded.

By now there was an urgent need for lift for the wounded; indeed Major Farrar-Hockley had been calling for casualty evacuation for more than an hour. The first helicopter despatched was pounced on and shot down by two Pucaras just after it left Camilla Creek House, the pilot, Lieutenant Richard Nunn, being killed, but other machines were soon on their way. The Pucaras, being piston-engined machines, had a distinctive sound all of their own. Designed for ground attack they could, when deftly handled, be quite a menace, but in their turn they were comparatively slow and thus vulnerable to small arms fire and Blowpipe.

Once A Company's wounded had been attended to, Lance-Corporal Framingham and Private O'Rourke began treating the wounded among the prisoners. They had to take forty shell-dressings from their comrades for the task, and did their best to treat the Argentines with as much care as their own men. The senior Argentine officer, who had fought most courageously, now did everything he could to ensure the good conduct of his men. There were six officers in all among the prisoners, most of whom were Special Forces, and these were the only officers the battalion found in the front line during the fighting. A padre was there too, and Sergeant Barrett called him over to adminster Last Rites to two of the badly wounded Argentines.

By now more helicopters were arriving and Captain Hughes, the MO, had come forward to treat the more urgent cases. Once A Company's wounded had been evacuated, Sergeant Barrett and his men began to help the Argentine stretcher cases into the helicopters.

The surrender had its moment of tragedy..After most of the enemy had laid down their arms one Argentine soldier walked forward, still holding a weapon in his hand. The men of 1 Platoon shouted to him to drop his gun, but instead he raised it to the aim. He was immediately shot and killed. Apart from this one incident the enemy behaved well. They were soon made glad of hot cups of tea, and the wounded were further helped by covering them with clothing taken from other, better-clad prisoners. The importance of magnanimity after battle had been stressed by Colonel 'H', and was now insisted upon by the company commander.

Although the area was still being shelled and mortared, the A Company battle for Darwin Hill was over. The enemy positions had been held by ninety-two men, of whom eighteen had been killed and thirty-nine wounded, (although some enemy had escaped from the farthest trenches) and the trenches had been most professionally sited, thoroughly protected and plentifully stocked with all types of ammunition. A Company had suffered three dead and twelve wounded, and three others—Colonel Jones, Captain Wood, and Corporal Melia—had also been killed. Their action had lasted for more than three hours, but they had cleared the eastern flank and now dominated the settlement at Darwin.

Throughout A Company's battle, B Company, after their initial attempt to take the Boca House position, had been waiting with most of the men on the reverse slope, but with their GPMGs, snipers and OPs keeping the enemy under fire wherever and whenever they could be engaged. It was obvious that any further frontal attack in daylight was unlikely to succeed, and that greatly increased fire support or a different axis of attack was required if the position was to be taken. The B Company soldiers had seen numbers of Argentines leaving their positions in front of A Company, but they had not then realised that these men were coming out to surrender to A Company. At that range they had no means of engaging them, which was fortunate since, had they done so, the surrender would have been jeopardised.

Within the battalion, the system of command had been carefully worked out so that at any time the second-in-command would know exactly what was going on. Now, with the CO dead, Major Chris Keeble was informed and he came forward to take over with the minimum of delay, anxious to regather the momentum of the advance. His immediate and urgent task was to sum up the situation, make a new plan, and get it swiftly into operation. Perhaps it was not so much a new plan that was needed, but a tidying-up and a renewal of emphasis on the original one, for in fact Major Neame with his D Company had intitially been briefed to pass through B Company, thus continuing the assault against the Boca House positions. Keeble had been able to speak to the Battery Commander and to John Crosland, and he now told the latter to take operational command until he himself was able to get up to the forward companies. Meanwhile the new CO collected as much ammunition as he and his group could possibly carry and then set off, and he also ordered the support platoons to get up to the ridge, where the four companies were now positioned, with all possible speed.

Major Keeble's orders and actions were enough to start things. Neame had already had his eye on the route along the western shore of the isthmus, where it looked as though a cliff edge would give cover from the Argentine Boca House complex. He therefore grouped most of his machine-guns together and directed them to a position from which they would be able to do much damage to the enemy, while he prepared to lead the rest of the company, crawling on their stomachs, round the beach, to take the enemy in the seaward flank and from the rear.

B Company, in the lee of the ridge, made ready to take advantage of this manoeuvre, preparing to attack once more when the D Company assault went in—the Boca House position would thus suffer a two-company attack from different quarters. As all this was happening, Chris Keeble came on the scene. He called a temporary halt to the companies' operations until the ammunition he had brought with him could be distributed and the support weapons placed in position, particularly the Milans, for the well prepared enemy bunkers badly needed attention from accurate direct-fire weapons, which could have a telling shock effect.

The death of the commanding officer in battle is bound to have a considerable impact, since so much depends upon his decisions, and because everyone in a battalion becomes accustomed to a particular way in which command is exercised. In a modern battle the CO will be almost continuously linked to his subordinates on the radio; they will hear his orders as he gives them and will hear any responses that other subordinates may make. 'H' Jones had been a particularly forceful and determined commander, and not a very easy man to live up to. But in a good battalion everything continues to work, no matter what disasters occur, and so it was with 2 Para. Everyone knew that things would be different, but nothing would interfere with the machinery. Now nothing must stop the momentum.

With the ammunition distributed and the support weapons in place, Major Philip Neame and his company were soon on their way, with their machine-guns, grouped under the command of 2nd Lieutenant Chris Waddington, positioned to cover them. As had been thought, most of the route was out of sight of the Argentine Boca House positions and they were able to make good progress, for the steep little cliff along the shore gave excellent cover. The going was firm and they were grateful that no mines had been laid. At high tide the water came right up to the bottom of the cliff and it was approaching that now.

Then, back on the ridge, Milan was brought into action. This anti-tank rocket can be dead accurate up to 2,000 yards, especially against a stationary target, and now the enemy bunkers could be clearly seen. Two direct hits were scored almost immediately and this, combined with the effects of the massed machine-gun fire, brought signs of the wish to surrender from the enemy. As Crosland, who was watching, described it, 'Milan was like Anadin as a pain-killer to our own people, and the reverse to the Argies,' and the CO said later, 'It really upset them. It was almost the beginning of the end.'

The machine-gunners and B Company, on the former's immediate left, were, however, still under fire from elsewhere, and were suffering casualties. Corporal Margerison, who had done so well during the night's fighting, had been badly wounded, and was with a little group beneath the ridge, anxiously waiting to be evacuated. For Major Crosland the immediate handling of affairs was not easy: any attempt to move over the ridge was met with accurate fire; it was necessary to keep the enemy engaged until the move round to the rear of the positions had been completed, yet some of the Argentines in the nearer positions were already showing white flags or the equivalent; and it was difficult to control the machine-gunners, who were all very keen on continuing action. 'Are we never going to have a go at them?' was the plaintive query raised by one of them, just as the company commander's stern and definite order came—'Cease firing'.

Suddenly the white flags were definitely out as D Company left the beach to storm into and through the Argentine positions.

It was all deftly managed and, with the minimum possible delay, Neame's men were up in the Boca House complex, clearing the bunkers and rounding up the prisoners. They counted twelve dead and took fifteen captive, some of whom were severely wounded. The unwounded Argentines were made to lie face down on the grass until the Company Sergeant-Major was on the scene to take charge of them. A mine had been set off as the company was making its final approach and this had added to the general excitement, stirred further by one of the machine-guns being afflicted with 'runaway gun' at a particularly delicate period.

D Company's action paved the way to the capture of the high ground dominating Goose Green, and would facilitate the destruction of the Darwin and Schoolhouse garrisons if the enemy were still in those places. But Major Neame knew that he must exploit his success as far as possible, and he therefore pressed on with his company without pausing to reorganise.

By now Keeble had a real grip of the battle, and was issuing clear orders to the companies. A Company was to stay where it was on Darwin Hill, but would make one of its platoons available to C Company who, having first completed making good all the high ground above the settlement, would clear Darwin. D Company would continue moving forward up to high ground dominating the airfield, and would deal with the enemy known to be in the Schoolhouse. B Company was to make a wide flanking movement to the south to block Goose Green off from that direction. Thus by the end of these manoeuvres the enemy would be bottled up in Goose Green, with the battalion overlooking them from three sides. There was still no firm information as to the strength of the enemy in Darwin itself, although it was thought that there might be a company in the Schoolhouse. The first task, therefore, was the clearance of Darwin and the interrogation of the prisoners, in the hopes of learning more about the enemy dispositions. One point was proved, however. Two Argentine Special Forces officers taken earlier admitted that, following the BBC announcement the day before of the impending attack on Darwin and Goose Green, up to three companies of fresh troops had been brought into the area. (Their story was corroborated some two weeks later when the battalion eventually arrived in Stanley. The local librarian had kept a diary of arrivals and departures by helicopter to and from the race-course: on 27 May up to 500 men had left for Goose Green by Chinook.)

Support Company was now positioned to be able to back up all the rifle companies, but there were still only two mortars available, and precious little ammunition for these. Keeble had Major Rice, the Battery Commander, with him, together with Major Hector Gullan, the Brigade Liaison Officer, but there were still only the three 105-mm guns available, and there could be no naval gun support until after dark. Requests for Harrier support had not so far been accepted; indeed, with the rather confused nature of the fighting, it had not been easy to 'task' them—provide targets for the aircraft—without endangering part of the battalion. The accuracy and effectiveness of the three guns in support had been disappointing. It takes time to achieve first-class co-operation between different arms in battle and in this case the two units—2 Para and the Royal Artillery battery—had never even seen each other before, so that it is not surprising that the outcome was imperfect.

As regards administration during the battle, the QM(Tech), Captain Banks Middleton, had been doing what he could throughout the day to maintain a re-supply forward from 'B' Echelon back at San Carlos. The battalion's survival depended upon this tenuous chain. Fortunately the co-location of 'B' Echelon with the naval air squadrons helped, and Banks's team was always able to have a netted load ready to go. The system of requests for support helicopters, however, did little to improve the back-up to the battalion, since all movements had first to be sanctioned by Brigade. In the event, just enough supplies went forward to 'A' Echelon at Camilla Creek House, although this was more by good luck than design. Nothing could better illustrate the need for dedicated support helicopters, actually grouped to the battalion and available at its call throughout an operation.

Similarly, the lack of vehicles was critical. The battalion had had to depend on the one Landrover captured at Camilla Creek House, in which Sergeant Pye and Lance-Corporal Thayer had done wonders ferrying mortar ammunition forward and taking walking wounded back. At some time in the morning a little 'airborne initiative' was applied. Two Royal Corps of Transport Snowcat drivers sitting on Sussex Mountain were hijacked, much to their surprise, turned to the south and told to get moving in their vehicles. In the night to come they were to prove invaluable, for the first-line ammunition scales—that is, the ammunition actually carried by the soldiers—had long been expended.

Prisoners were now being marched back to Camilla Creek House under Sergeant Spencer of the Defence Platoon. Once there, they were as well looked-after as the conditions allowed. They were provided with peat for fires to keep warm in the sheep pens, and that night were moved upstairs into the house itself: tightly bunched, perhaps, but far better than being left in the bitter cold outside. They were fed as well as possible in the rather spartan circumstances prevailing.

Meanwhile the RAP had been split into two groups, with Captain Hughes's party behind A Company and Captain Rory Wagon's group behind B. The availability of a second doctor proved a godsend, for to have had to concentrate all the B Company casualties down to the A Company's position in the gorse gully would have been a monumental task, and would have meant a painful journey for the wounded.

With the Boca House position cleared C Company now began to clear Darwin itself, but there was a change of plan and the company was switched to moving forward towards the airfield from the gorse-line. Meanwhile D Company had begun its move towards the airfield and B Company had started its long loop down the west of the isthmus, while A Company, less its one platoon detached to C, reorganised in the gulley.

C Company broke the skyline with the Milan and machine-guns just behind them, heading down the long slope towards the Schoolhouse. Lieutenant Connor's Recce Platoon was on the left, Captain Farrar's Patrol Platoon on the right and Wallis's 3 Platoon from A Company in reserve, the Paras moving in extended line with bayonets fixed. To Corporal Evans in the Recce Platoon, the scene evoked images of the battles of the First World War: all that was needed was the blast on the whistle to go over the top. He could see the enemy standing on the airfield, apparently immobilised by the sight.

Major Roger Jenner, his company commander, could see D Company away to the right, moving from Boca House towards the airfield in the relative safety that the re-entrant afforded. The enemy suddenly realised what was happening and ran to the

Oerlikons, which they brought into action against C Company—as Jenner later described it: 'You could feel the guns zeroing in on you.' He called for artillery support, but none was available.

One of the machine-gunners, Private Russell, was knocked over as the wave of shells reached the hillside. Major Jenner, although wounded himself, ran over to give him encouragement and to see if he was all right, while his signaller, Private Holman-Smith, offered to man the GPMG. As he moved forward to pick it up, however, Holman-Smith was killed by a shell from an Oerlikon on the airfield. Russell was badly wounded, and both the company commander and his other signaller had narrow escapes.

Jenner dressed the machine-gunner's wound while the intense fire continued. He called for a stretcher for Russell, and Sergeant-Major Peatfield's party came forward to pick him up. The company commander had suddenly lost radio contact with his platoons although he could see them moving forward below him.

Now enemy fire began coming from the Schoolhouse area and from the near edge of the airfield. Both C Company and, to the west, B Company were very exposed as they came over higher ground, and were vulnerable to all types of weapons from the dug-in Argentine positions beyond them. Within 3 Platoon, Privates Thomas and Tunn and Sergeant Beattie were all hit, and the platoon pulled back into cover. Then the two leading C Company platoons also went to ground, seeking cover on the open slope. They had been well spaced out, and so had taken few casualties.

Milan had been deployed on the left of C Company and snipers moved into the gorse-line to cover the airfield. The support machine-guns were ordered forward to within range of the Schoolhouse and Major Hugh Jenner, the Support Company commander, had moved his own command post so that he could watch both the airfield and the Schoolhouse, although it would take some time for his men to identify and then engage the enemy effectively.

Meanwhile, Neame's D Company was now well on its way towards the airfield, having dropped off Corporal Owen's section from 10 Platoon to clear Boca House and look after the wounded and prisoners. 12 Platoon was in the lead and racing ahead when its commander, Lieutenant Jim Barry, saw some Argentines pulling away from the airfield directly in front. He ordered Corporal Sullivan's section to open fire, which inflicted some casualties on the enemy. More Argentine troops headed down into dead ground towards the Schoolhouse, and disappeared out of sight. By moving diagonally south-east, Barry was able to avoid the Oerlikon fire from the airfield, and the protection of the valley leading to the Schoolhouse was sufficient to allow a left hook around the airfield towards the flagpole on the high ground where an Argentine flag was fluttering.

Enemy troops could now be seen running back across the footbridge down by the estuary towards the Schoolhouse, while others ran towards the flagpole. Neame saw what he thought might be a headquarters in a hollow on the high ground at the western end of the airfield, and he sent Lieutenant Shaun Webster to take it with his 10 Platoon.

Webster could see no enemy on the airfield itself as he and his two sections moved forward to the hollow. It was obviously a command post which had been abandoned by the enemy, who had plainly withdrawn in a hurry. But as 10 Platoon moved up it came under fire from the south-west, and Webster therefore decided on a left flanking attack, leaving Corporal Stadden's section to give support. With his platoon headquarters and Corporal Elliott's section he went into the assault, but as the Paras charged towards a second line of abandoned enemy trenches on the runway, they suddenly came under very heavy fire from what may have been a complete platoon position along the south side of the runway. Fire poured down on Webster's small party from the left and right, and they took cover in the trenches so conveniently to hand.

The enemy position was in a banked-up area near the flagpole. Over the radio the company commander told Webster not to attempt to go further but to get into a fire position to cover the rest of the company, which would be making for the flagpole. At that point, suddenly and unexpectedly, machine-guns opened up on 10 Platoon—from behind! Everyone not already under cover leapt into the trenches as heavy and accurate bursts landed all around. This was not the enemy, however—this was machine-guns firing from positions near the gorse.

Gradually the fire decreased, and it was most fortunate that no one was hit. In an attempt to attract the machine-gunners' attention, the men of 10 Platoon put their distinctive red berets on their weapons and waved them in the air, while Webster tried to get through on the radio via Company HQ to persuade them to stop firing. Fortunately the Machine-Gun Platoon actually saw the berets and ceased fire. Webster regrouped his men and they followed on behind the company, but the incident had held them up for more than half-an-hour.

Meanwhile the company commander had moved round with 11 and 12 Platoons until they neared the estuary. All the time he found himself being pushed further and further to the left by the presence of a minefield on his right flank and thus was being forced towards the Schoolhouse and the track leading from it to Goose Green.

As his platoons approached, Neame noticed a number of enemy regrouping by the school, and it was obvious that these would have to be dealt with before anything else. Then the enemy in the Schoolhouse opened fire and Neame directed 11 Platoon into an assault from the creek whilst 12 Platoon was to provide covering fire from the track higher up the hill towards the flagpole. Before 12 Platoon had time to move, however, Lieutenant Barry noticed a number of white flags flying in the schoolhouse windows. He ordered Private Knight to tell Company HQ, but in the confusion the information did not get through, although Corporal Kincher also shouted over the air: 'They've got f—— white flags up there at the Schoolhouse.' Even so, fire was still coming from a number of enemy positions near the building, and thus it could not be presumed that a general surrender was being offered.

There now followed a rather confused but very hard-fought battle for the Schoolhouse and the other buildings in its immediate area. 11 Platoon of D Company was in the forefront, having been led up by the company commander, who now had to consider action by the rest of the company, which was being threatened by the enemy near the flagpole by the airfield. Now merging into the schoolhouse affray came C Company's Patrol Platoon, which had been on the left of D Company, with Captain Farrar and CSM Greenhalgh playing prominent parts in the action.

The buildings caught fire and dense black smoke added to the confusion, but there was no more sign of surrender here at this stage. Then the enemy on Goose Green Point took a hand, opening up with heavier weapons despite there still being Argentine soldiers in and around the Schoolhouse, some of whom were in dug-in positions around the buildings which had originally been sited for seaward defence. Enemy fire was also coming from positions on the airfield, and Neame was now trying to use his 12 Platoon to deal with them.

C and D Companies were suffering casualties now, among them Private Dixon, killed, and Lance-Corporal Tighe, wounded. Once again the white phosphorus grenades were found to be most effective in helping men to get close to the enemy, and gradually the Paras began to clear the positions. Then, suddenly, it was all over, and all opposition ceased. It is difficult to estimate the numbers that had been holding the Schoolhouse area. Afterwards a number of charred bodies were found, perhaps of Argentines who had been trying to hide and had been caught as buildings collapsed.

During the battle for the Schoolhouse, Lieutenant Barry saw what he thought to be a white flag in the area of the flagpole. He told his platoon sergeant, Sergeant Meredith, that he was going up to take a surrender, and Company HQ was informed. Neame was worried about this and forbade any such move until the Schoolhouse had been sorted out, but his instruction never reached Barry. Sergeant Meredith shouted for the platoon radio operator, Private Knight, to go up with the platoon commander, and Private Godfrey, the platoon runner, was already with Barry. Corporal Sullivan's section was ordered to follow.

About five enemy had approached, holding their weapons in both hands above their heads, as if to surrender. Godfrey stopped, sensing that something was wrong, and Corporal Sullivan ordered his machine-gun team to move forward to cover their platoon commander. Further to the right could be seen more bunkers, with enemy in them.

Corporal Sullivan called up to Knight, 'What's he doing now?'

'I don't know,' Knight shouted back, 'He must have gone mad!'

Their 'boss' was literally face to face with the five Argentines, who still held their weapons above their heads. One of the enemy had climbed over the fence. Suddenly he levelled his gun, gesticulating with it to Barry to drop his own weapon and surrender to them. The British officer, however, was trying to tell the soldier that he must put his weapon down, using his own to demonstrate his demand. Knight and Godfrey both got down. From behind a burst of tracer, possibly from the battle at the Schoolhouse, whipped over their heads. The enemy opened fire on Lieutenant Barry from point-blank range, and he was killed outright, as was Sullivan and Lance-Corporal Smith.

That is one version of the incident. According to Sergeant Meredith, however, two unarmed Argentines came forward towards Jim Barry, while another six or so stayed sitting down in cover. The two men had their hands in the air and one had a white handkerchief. They were pointing at the battle going on at the Schoolhouse below and ducking as odd rounds came over. Barry told Knight to get a grip on Company HQ to stop the firing, which would obviously jeopardise a surrender. He then moved as if to lean his weapon against the fence. A long burst of fire, probably from the Machine-Gun Platoon, came over their heads. The enemy behind and in the trenches suddenly opened fire and Barry was killed.

The conflicting accounts of what actually happened are typical of such incidents, for in the heat of battle men form different impressions. It will never be possible to establish the exact truth, though both accounts agree that fire was brought to bear towards the Argentines as Barry moved forward, and that he was shot down in a breach of good faith. The rule ought to be that those wishing to surrender should do the moving under cover of a white flag, while those appealed to should remain still, poised and able to accept or reject as circumstances demand.

After Jim Barry had been killed, there was a general exchange of fire in the area, and most of the Argentines began to make their way into Goose Green itself. Small groups were surrendering as and when they emerged from outlying positions around the edge of the airfield. Meanwhile Lieutenant Peter Kennedy, the C Company second-in-command, had come up to the flagpole and taken charge there. Various targets could be seen within the settlement, including some artillery that was still in action, but it was not easy to engage them in the gathering darkness. Nor was it going to be practical to mount any form of attack until much more information could be gathered about the enemy, particularly his strength, weapons and dispositions.

B Company had completed its long encircling move, and had taken up positions on and around a small piece of high ground immediately south-west of the settlement. D Company was re-grouped just north of the airfield, while C Company was concentrating near the gorse-line from which it had set out for the Schoolhouse; also in this general area were Support Company and Battalion HQ. At about this time there was an enemy air attack, one fast low run being made by two Skyhawks, using cannon to strafe B and D Companies. They caused no damage or casualties, however, and one of the aircraft was brought down. Another run was made by a Pucara, but it was downed by the Royal Marines Blowpipe detachment, which had moved forward to the gorse-line. The aircraft smashed into the hillside among the B Company positions, narrowly missing some of the men.

Earlier, just after 1800 hours, a request had been made for a Harrier strike against the enemy positions on the point, which were out of range of the support weapons and the artillery. At about 1925 hours, just after the enemy air attack, three RAF Harriers screamed over from the north-west to deliver a strike on the point at Goose Green. (It was probably a Sidewinder missile from one of these incoming aircraft that had destroyed the Argentine Skyhawk, since the air attacks virtually coincided.) To hit the enemy on the point was no easy task, for it was known that a number of British Falklanders had been incarcerated in some of the buildings of the settlement for several days, and one inaccurate bomb among these buildings could prove disastrous.

The enemy positions near the point, where there was also one 3.7-inch AA gun and some Oerlikons, were crucial, for weapons sited there could cover a very wide arc, and they were not easy to attack or to hit. 2 Para had earlier tried Milan, mortar and artillery fire, but to no avail since the range was too great, and the enemy's return fire had been heavy and accurate. Now the Harriers came in singly, dropping cluster bombs, and although not all were effective, the aircraft making the last run, this time from the north-east, seemed to score. Little more was heard from the enemy on the point after the Harriers had been over, although at least one 35-mm gun continued to fire. As it turned out, the strike by the last aircraft had caused considerable casualties, and a loud outcry from the garrison could be heard which continued well into the night. It seemed that morale among the Argentine soldiers attacked by the Harriers had been quite seriously affected.

Shortly afterwards, just before dark, another Pucara made a low-level run, sweeping in over D Company and dropping napalm canisters, which burnt furiously, though luckily harmlessly, near some of the 2 Para positions. B and D Companies turned every available weapon on the aircraft, which went out of control and crashed, showering B Company with fuel. The pilot baled out and was later captured, unharmed, by men of 12 Platoon.

Major Hector Gullan now went back to Brigade. It had been gathered from Mr Brooke Hardcastle, the Manager in Darwin, that there were 114 civilians incarcerated in Goose Green. They had been living for some weeks in very cramped and uncomfortable conditions, although without actually being ill treated. Nevertheless, all the real comforts had been denied them, which was perhaps unavoidable in the circumstances.

As the light began to fade, B Company, on the outskirts of Goose Green, suddenly saw a flight of enemy helicopters appear from the south and begin to put down troops about 1,000 metres south of the settlement. The flight comprised one Chinook and six Hueys, and was therefore carrying a good number of reinforcements. Calling for support from the gun-line, B Company moved to engage the disembarking troops—seconds later accurate artillery fire fell among the enemy soldiers. The flight immediately made off in a southerly direction, with the rest of its troops still aboard, apparently having no intention of becoming involved with the local battle. This was a considerable relief: there is something very threatening about the delivery of fresh reinforcements by air, just when the deleterious effects of a long and arduous battle are beginning to show.

Now Chris Keeble could take stock of the situation. He had his enemy nicely bottled up in the settlement, with his own companies, which he had pulled back into dead ground, all round the exits from Goose Green, on the higher ground above the settlement. The enemy had been shown to be able to fight a great deal better than had been suggested, particularly in daylight when they were in prepared positions with plenty of ammunition. Now all those defences had been overrun, however, the airfield with its heavy defences had been taken, and all that remained to the Argentines were whatever positions they could manage to improvise on the outskirts of the settlement during the night. Nevertheless, with the numbers available, the enemy should be capable of launching a counter-attack to regain their lost positions, or at least of effecting a damaging sortie. Given reasonable leadership, a stalwart foe would now be getting ready to do either of these things. In addition, the companies, especially B and D, were low in ammunition, water and rations, and the RAPs were full of casualties, Argentine as well as British.

The battalion had settled down very well since the death of the CO, and the whole machinery of command was working smoothly. The casualties had not been heavy, but everyone was beginning to feel really tired. There had been several days of tension and discomfort, some of it acute, and now all the comforts and protective clothing were still away on Sussex Mountain. Men could rest without these, but really deep refreshing sleep was impossible.

Probably feet were causing more trouble than anything else. Nearly everyone had got their feet soaked in salt water on the landing-craft several days ago and, however hard they tried and however often they changed their socks, it was almost impossible to eradicate the effects of that initial immersion of the boots. The Army boot was definitely not waterproof and now, as the men walked across rain-sodden, muddy ground covered in wet vegetation, the damp came in. Cold, clammy, wet feet, continuously nagging, debar almost anyone from feeling relaxed, but no one could afford the luxury of taking off their wet boots and changing into warm, dry socks.

All through the long, dark night the soldiers huddled together for warmth when and where they could, their positions alive with the disturbed noises of armed and anxious men, wondering about what exactly had happened during the previous hours, and what was going to happen during the next. Many had lost comrades through death, wounds or separation. There was the odd burst of machine-gun, artillery or mortar fire, from anywhere over the erstwhile battlefield. In places fires were still burning, occasionally spreading to discarded ammunition with a resulting cacophony of disturbing sound. Elsewhere, officers and men were moving to link up again, having become detached in the fighting, and there were calls for locations and identifications. 2 Para's dead, including the body of Lieutenant-Colonel 'H' Jones, had been collected and brought safely into the battalion area at dusk.

There were many wounded still to be evacuated and the helicopter lift was overloaded and overworked. The two Snowcats that had been hijacked were kept at it all night, moving between Camilla Creek House and the forward positions. There seemed to be a lack of understanding at Brigade of the battalion's predicament.

At that time 2 Para was the only part of the Commando Brigade that had been in action, and one would have thought that the utmost priority would have been given to its needs. Yet forward supplies of ammunition, food and all other rations were sadly missing, and facilities for casualty evacuation were not always available. In that cold, dark, wet atmosphere, the condition of any wounded in the forward area soon became distressful, and this could have had a most adverse effect on the morale of those who remained.

In a way, this was aggravated by a ruling that once a wounded man was evacuated to SS *Uganda*, the hospital ship, he was inevitably out of battle for the rest of the campaign, sent back to the UK, and had no chance of rejoining the battalion for several months. To many of the staunch old members of a fighting battalion this would be a most deplorable fate. There were some who refused to declare their wounds and tried to depend upon their comrades to see them through—indeed, the training on board ship had given many men a feeling of confidence in their ability to sustain and tend their own.

Evacuation by helicopter did, however, continue. Captain John Greenhalgh of the Army Air Corps Flight was a leading light in this respect, volunteering to come up time after time.*
One pilot caused trouble by refusing to pick up one of the Argentine wounded, for the enemy were being given as much

---

* Captain Greenhalgh was later awarded the Distinguished Flying Cross for his skilful and persistent efforts to recover casualties under fire during the battles for Darwin and Goose Green.

help as possible by the battalion system, but this little difficulty was soon cleared up. Rain was falling almost continuously, and everyone was longing for the contents of their bergen packs, still stacked away back on Sussex Mountain.

In the meantime, Chris Keeble had furiously to think. He knew that there were more than 100 civilians being held as prisoners in the settlement, and that therefore an all-out attack was not a possible course of action until every other means had been tried. He had been able to discuss matters with the Brigade Commander, who had offered him a Commando company as reinforcement, but Major Keeble knew that what he had to do was to arrange a surrender of the remaining Argentine garrison. He knew, too, that this would need most delicate handling in view of the relative strengths. But he sought and obtained from Brigade HQ the promise of reinforcements, three more artillery pieces with sufficient ammunition for a major assault, the rest of the battalion's mortars, rations and small arms ammunition, and, above all, vehicles and helicopters for the evacuation of the wounded. The Brigadier also agreed that, if it was absolutely necessary, the settlement might have to be destroyed in a full battalion attack.

Major Gullan, the Brigade Liaison Officer, had managed to keep Brigade fully informed of the course of events throughout the battle. But with so much at stake after so much had been achieved, it seems strange that the Brigadier did not come up himself to discuss things with Keeble who, one might say, had the most mighty problem that ever weighed down a temporary battalion commander upon his shoulders. The Brigadier was, of course, required to communicate almost continuously with the authorities in the UK, which must have made it difficult for him to leave his post. Nevertheless it is an established maxim within all that is best in the Army that every commander should visit his immediately subordinate units once a day, especially during battle, whatever the difficulties. In this case, if the Liaison Officer could go back to Brigade, then the Brigade Commander should have been able to come forward.

Anyway, Keeble's intention was to make contact with the enemy, and in this he was much helped by the Brigadier, who sent a message via Alan Miller, the farm manager at Port San Carlos, to Eric Goss, the farm manager at Goose Green, to say that two Argentine prisoners would be despatched to the enemy HQ in Goose Green in the morning.

Under Keeble's direction, Captain Coulson, the IO, and Rod Bell spent much of the night writing an ultimatum in Spanish. Keeble spoke to one prisoner via Bell's interpretation, making certain that he at least appreciated the fate in store for any Argentine force that tried to resist an attack by 2 Para. He himself was quite confident in the ability of the battalion to storm the settlement. The utter discomfort that he and his men were suffering was sufficient guarantee that nothing could prevent them getting under proper cover before another day was out. He had good reason to be more than satisfied with the sheer skill and abilities of the battalion. There had been mistakes, of course, and some of his components were stronger than others, but no one could doubt the fighting qualities of his men.

'H' Jones, his own CO of only a few hours ago, had set a most outstanding example. He had shown that 2 Para was just not stoppable. His example and his indelible spirit would stay and permeate the battalion throughout the campaign. And so, if it should be necessary, in the morning the battalion would roll forward once again. For his leadership and courage throughout the battle, Lieutenant-Colonel Herbert Jones was posthumously awarded the Victoria Cross.

CHAPTER 5

Victory—and After

Saturday, 29 May—a misty start to the day, with visibility much restricted. During the night Keeble had selected two Argentine NCOs, who had been suitably brainwashed as to the strength and ferocity of his own forces, and at 1000 hours these were sent under a white flag into Goose Green to contact the enemy headquarters. They took with them the ultimatum, in English and Spanish, and they were to request that, as the Argentine position was so hopeless, their leaders should come forward to parley.* Under the terms of the ultimatum, if the prisoners returned under a white flag then a parley would take place, but if they returned without such a flag then the enemy was not prepared to negotiate. If the two NCOs did not return within one hour then 2 Para would attack. In fact, the prisoners returned almost as soon as they entered the settlement—a rendezvous between 2 Para and the Argentine leaders had been fixed for later in the day.

In the meantime reinforcements, in the shape of J Company, 42 RM Commando, were coming in, the other three 105-mm guns of the battery and the battalion's remaining 81-mm mortars had been helicoptered to the gun-line at Camilla Creek House, with plentiful stocks of ammunition, and the Harrier force had been put at priority availability. If there should be further doubts in Argentine minds about the fire-power that he could now command, Keeble intended to stage a demonstration well within

---

* The text of Major Keeble's ultimatum is given in Appendix IV.

the view of the enemy garrison. He felt that he was becoming stronger all the time, and that therefore a little delay would do no harm. But he could not help wishing that the Scorpion and Scimitar tanks of the Blues and Royals, which he had been most anxious to have for the operation, were available now. The threat of the use of armour could have been a considerable factor in helping the Argentines to make up their minds.

At the agreed time, around midday, Keeble set off for the rendezvous with the enemy envoys. His party consisted of Major Rice, the Battery Commander, Major Gullan, the Brigade LO, Captain Bell as interpreter, and Corporal Shaw, a radio operator, and also included, as civilian witnesses, the two war correspondents, David Norris of the *Daily Mail* and Robert Fox of the BBC. The latter spoke Italian and had considerable knowledge of Italian people (many Argentines are of Italian extraction), and his advice to Keeble was to heed their innate desire to save 'face', in that, if they could be made to feel they had fought well, honour would be satisfied and they would the more readily lay down their arms. The rain turned to hail as the party moved past large amounts of abandoned equipment, and there were minefields about, with dead, bloated cattle much in evidence. There was a considerable air of tension.

The agreed meeting-place was a corrugated iron hut on the west side of the airfield, with a white flag flying outside it. Standing patrols from A and D Companies provided cover as the unarmed British party entered the hut, and in due course the enemy party arrived. An Argentine naval officer conducted the niceties, introducing the Garrison Commander, Air Vice-Commodore Wilson Dosio Pedroza, and the Army Commander, Lieutenant-Colonel Italo Pioggi, a small, deeply tanned soldier.

Keeble began by stressing his concern for the welfare of the inhabitants, and the Argentines readily agreed to their release. It was clear that the Air Vice-Commodore was willing to come to terms immediately, but that the Colonel wanted more time to consult General Menendez in Stanley by radio. Hector Gullan said that there would soon have to be an end to prevarication and that General Menendez would know that the men in Goose Green had fought well but were now in a very dangerous situation, and Rod Bell impressed upon the enemy commanders the dire consequences if they did not surrender. The Colonel wanted to lay down conditions about the evacuation of his troops from the battle zone and their subsequent repatriation, whilst Keeble was insisting on assurances about the safety of the Falklanders.

The headquarters of D Company, just over the brow of a rise in the ground, reported that a number of Argentines were making their way into the settlement. These must have been the men helicoptered in just before last light on the previous day, and orders were given to the effect that they were not to be prevented from moving in to Goose Green. When asked about the minefields, it transpired that the leaders had no idea where they had been laid—the mines had simply been scattered about by a corporal, entirely unrecorded. It was decided between the two parties that if a surrender was to take place then the Argentines would come forward to a chosen site at a specified time.

The Argentine commanders then returned to the settlement while Keeble and his party tried to keep warm, anxiously waiting for the next move, not knowing whether they would have to fight yet again. They could see over a hedge into Goose Green, where there seemed to be considerable activity, including signs of men packing kit. At 1310 hours they moved forward to the edge of a fairly extensive piece of open ground at the top of the settlement, which had been selected as the site for surrender if one was going to take place, just as some 250 Argentine Air Force men commanded by Wilson Pedroza came out and formed up. Pedroza then made an impassioned harangue, after which the Argentine National Anthem was sung. The men then laid down their arms, and Pedroza turned to Keeble, saluted, and handed over his belt and pistol. The airmen were then allowed to slope off back to their feeding place for a meal.

So far, so good, but where were the soldiers? And then, suddenly, a considerable hubbub began as men literally poured out of the buildings to converge on the open ground. There seemed to be no end to them and eventually perhaps 1,000 were paraded. Taking into account the numbers already accounted for, here was proof that the strength of the enemy in the peninsula must have been considerably more than the figure given in intelligence reports before the battle. The soldiers, many of them in rather bad physical shape and some poorly clad, grounded arms with less ceremony than the airmen. This time the Regimental Sergeant-Major took charge of the prisoners, and they were kept in a body, guarded by D Company, until firm decisions could be made as to where and how these much larger numbers could be accommodated and administered. The senior officers were flown off to Brigade HQ without further delay, and Major Keeble moved on to the community hall to release the jubilant civilians. At 1450 hours the surrender terms were formally agreed—it was all over*.

2 Para could, at last, relax. Off came the helmets and the war paint, then a good clean-up was, as ever, the first item on the programme. Now the soldiers were able to wander about among the buildings, talking to the lately released inhabitants and hearing about their weeks of captivity. Apparently some of the enemy had been sympathetic, even kindly, but others had been cruel and vicious. The Argentines had made a point of destroying any radio equipment they came across, and they had greatly feared the islanders being able to communicate with other settlements, or to send information to Stanley. Most trying, perhaps, was their primitive attitude to sanitation and Western European culture was sadly lacking in this respect. Once the inhabitants of Goose Green had been incarcerated in the community hall, they had formed a committee to deal with their affairs and to keep contact with the Argentines. Before long, adequate arrangements existed for feeding, sleeping and passing the time. The farm manager, Eric Goss, had been allowed to stay in his house, and he had thus been able to keep an eye on properties from which the owners had been expelled.

The parachutist is always fascinated by other nations' weapons. Perhaps this is partly because he is in greater danger than the ordinary soldier of running out of ammunition, and therefore likes to be able to make use of captured enemy weapons. It was not long after the battle, therefore, that all the captured Argentine small arms were being thoroughly tested. Padre David Cooper is, as has been said, a crack Bisley marksman and he was well to the fore in looking for something

---

* That morning a television camera crew had come forward to film the surrender. In the event, however, Major Keeble, in consultation with others, decided that their presence might jeopardise the delicate negotiations, and the crew was kept occupied by Major Miller, the Operations Officer, while the surrender was discussed.

that might improve the performance of the battalion's snipers. The resultant outbursts of firing were a little disturbing to the local people, and to the captives, for that matter, since all were now looking forward to a period of peace and quiet.

The little settlement was, and is, a rather lovely place, and the greenness of the land and the abundance of geese confirmed the aptness of its name. The hills of Lafonia Island to the south seemed particularly beguiling, and when the winds dropped while the sun shone it was a place that all could feel had been well worth fighting for. It never takes long for a parachute battalion to recover from hardship, and it was most pleasant for the British troops now to be able to discuss the battle in retrospect, and to begin to look forward to the next event.

2 Para casualties had been fifteen killed and thirty wounded.* It was estimated that 250 enemy had been killed and at least that number wounded, with well over 1,000 captured unwounded. The booty included four 105-mm pack howitzers, two 35-mm AA guns, six 20-mm AA guns, six 120-mm mortars, two Pucara aircraft and large quantities of ammunition, with other stores of all kinds. It was a classic victory.

Two days later, Major Chris Keeble, the six company commanders, the Padre and the RSM were flown back to Ajax Bay to see the battalion's dead buried, in a large pit that had been bulldozed by the Sappers out of the hillside above San Carlos Water. It was a simple little ceremony conducted by the Padre, David Cooper. There were no bugles or firing party, and at the end the Paras and the other soldiers present saluted, while RSM Simpson scattered a handful of earth over the bodies. Even classic victories have their price.

---

* The Roll of Honour of officers and men of the battalion killed in action in the Falklands is included in Appendix I.

CHAPTER 6

Fitzroy and Bluff Cove

The ordeals of the civilian populations of Goose Green and Darwin settlements are part of another story. It is enough to say that they were very delighted to see the battalion, and that the battalion was equally glad to see that not one of them had been harmed in the fighting. The business of clearing up the settlement was to take weeks rather than days, and the real credit for this necessary task lies elsewhere, with other troops brought in to handle the job.

2 Para sorely needed a respite to allow men to dry out and to recover. Even so, the acting CO was already busy planning ahead for the next operation. There were thought to be several isolated Argentine observation posts in the vicinity and plans were made for finding and dealing with them.

The battalion was now virtually independent. 3 Commando Brigade had moved to the northern route and Headquarters, Landing Force Falkland Islands (LFFI) was not yet established, so the battalion had no contact with any higher command. Since 29 May a part of 5 Infantry Brigade had been on *Norland*, moving from South Georgia to Port San Carlos (the rest of the brigade was on board SS *Canberra*, also heading for San Carlos Water) and ably assisted in their embarkation and disembarkation by Tom Godwin's team, still on board. Co-operation had been excellent, and during the long night of 1 June 1/7th Gurkha Rifles was put on shore at Ajax Bay, to be followed by the remainder of 'B' Echelon. At last the battalion was completely ashore.

101

Supply to Goose Green was haphazard. Fortunately the co-location of the helicopter squadron and 'B' Echelon helped considerably, especially since Godwin had a plentiful supply of paraffin heaters: it was amazing how well a barter economy could work in getting additional flights! Gradually the much-needed re-supply of the battalion was effected.

The smooth flow of events at Goose Green was marred by one major tragedy. On the evening of 2 June a huge explosion rent the air. Argentine prisoners who had been clearing large piles of ammunition had become the victims of what was thought to be their own booby trap. Although the movement of war stocks by prisoners-of-war is normally regarded as a breach of the Geneva Convention, in this particular instance the Argentines had actually asked to move the ammunition owing to its nearness to the large black wool-shed that was now doing duty as a prisoner-of-war cage.

The damage was horrendous. Nine prisoners were badly burnt, three were dead, of whom one had been seen burning in the flames. Sergeant Fowler, the Medical Sergeant, had rushed to the scene, but his attempts to drag the burning torso out of the flames were in vain. To save the unfortunate victim from further suffering, he shot the remains—the most humanitarian course of action he could take.

The casualties were treated by Captains Hughes and Wagon at the RAP. Once a Chinook became available, Wagon went back to Ajax Bay with the patients, where they were given immediate treatment. One man who had had both his legs blown off died later on the operating table, but the remaining prisoners lived, thanks to the speed of their evacuation and the promptness of the action taken.

The field hospital was becoming short of blood for the wounded, and Wagon therefore approached the senior Argentine Air Force officer for contributions from among the prisoners. At first he refused, but when he was shown that the men of the surgical teams were trying to help he gave way, and ordered all the fit prisoners to volunteer. He then gave further information about other booby traps at Goose Green. These were found in some of the houses and shelters—each having to be carefully removed by the Sappers.

The gruesome task of the collection and counting of the enemy dead remained. David Cooper, the Padre, tried to work with the senior Argentine officer so as to ensure proper identification of bodies before burial. The officer showed little inclination to co-operate, however, adamantly insisting that he had a complete list of those killed and that he would take full responsibility. The Padre had to take the officer's sincerity on trust. The dead, meanwhile, were concentrated into groups along the track that had been the battalion centre-line during the battle.

On 31 May Major-General Jeremy Moore, now the overall commander for the land forces, had landed at San Carlos and his HQ, LFFI was now in operation, commanding the two brigades and their back-up. The leading elements of 5 Brigade had also begun to arrive in the San Carlos beach-head on the 31st, headed by Brigadier Tony Wilson in his helicopter, and 2 Para now came under his command, as it had done in the UK.* The question facing all was what should be done next, as 3 Commando Brigade was nearing the enemy positions to the east of Stanley after a long slog across the north of the island.

Back at Darwin settlement, Major Dair Farrar-Hockley's A Company was still dug in near its battlefield. Dair had talked to the local inhabitants, and in particular to Brooke Hardcastle, regarding future moves. The Darwin Manager suggested that someone should telephone some friends of his at Bluff Cove and Fitzroy, Kevin Hannaway, who lived in the former settlement, and Ron Binney, in the latter.

The capture of both settlements had attractions. Located to the south of Mount Kent, they were just visible from the enemy-held feature of Mount Harriet. Fitzroy had the advantage of a good harbour and jetty, large wool-sheds for storage, and all the essential facilities such as water, electricity and houses for shelter.

The idea was put to Chris Keeble, who immediately accepted it. Here was a chance to find, at an instant, the disposition of all enemy forces on the southern route between Goose Green and Stanley. A party was sent to Burntside House, in the hope of finding the telephone lines intact, but they were down.

---

* 5 Infantry Brigade in the Falklands comprised 2nd Scots Guards, 1st Welsh Guards, and 1/7th (Duke of Edinburgh's Own) Gurkha Rifles, together with a troop of the Blues and Royals, artillery, engineers, medical and signals units and other brigade troops.

It was then decided to try another settlement at Swan Inlet, some miles further east, where it was thought there might be a working telephone. 6 Platoon of B Company had been on standby for a raid on Mount Usborne to destroy an enemy observation post believed to be located there, so it was the obvious choice for the Swan Inlet operation. Once more Captain John Greenhalgh came to the help of the battalion with an additional three Scout helicopters, making five available in all, of which two were fitted with SS-11 missiles.

Major John Crosland's plan was to fly to rendezvous south of the settlement and then to approach the buildings at ground level. The SS-11s would be fired and then three assault helicopters, each containing four men, would land in a triangular formation, with the company commander at the apex, Lieutenant Chapman's group on the left and Corporal Bradford's group on the right.

On 2 June the force took off and the assault went in. The SS-11s were fired and one exploded, demolishing two of the buildings ahead, although the other two missiles became 'rogue' and flew off harmlessly. The helicopters landed to find the area deserted.

John Crosland and the Intelligence Section Colour Sergeant, Alan Morris, found the telephone and gave it two turns on the old-fashioned hand crank. A voice at the other end in Fitzroy—Ron Binney's—replied. Explaining who they were, they asked if any enemy were in Fitzroy or Bluff Cove; the answer was in the negative, although the bridge at Fitzroy had been tampered with. 'We'll be seeing you shortly', said John and rang off.

The news was radioed to Major Chris Keeble back at Goose Green: 'Fleet and Balham are clear.' (The choice of nickname was fairly typical: John Crosland lived in Fleet in Hampshire, and Balham, according to a famous comic monologue, is the 'gateway to the south'!) The B Company party then returned to their helicopters.

Brigadier Tony Wilson, who had been planning a five-day cross-country move to Fitzroy, quickly squashed this in favour of a helicopter leap-frog by 2 Para, and the move began later on Wednesday, 2 June. The usual lack of helicopters was the main difficulty and there was only one Chinook available* to move the entire battalion, apart from the small Scout helicopters with their limited fuel, range and lift.

It was already nearly dusk when the leading elements took off after a hurried 'O' Group in the Community hall. A Company Headquarters with two platoons, plus B Company Headquarters with one platoon and some mortar and anti-tank detachments spearheaded the move in the Chinook. Ahead of these groups, Scout helicopters had inserted two patrols of the Patrol Platoon into Bluff Cove, and two patrols from Recce into Fitzroy, to confirm the absence of Argentines and to mark the landing-sites for the main body.

Mount Kent had been captured by elements of 3 Commando Brigade on the day before. These troops had already been *in situ* for some time, and did not know that the helicopters landing to their south were friendly. Captain Rod Jenkins, one of the FOOs on Mount Kent, was about to begin shelling when he suddenly realised from the helicopter markings that these were British troops being landed at Fitzroy and Bluff Cove. Luckily he was able to stop the guns in time.

When Captain Greenhalgh's helicopters returned from dropping off the Patrol and Recce parties, they had exhausted their flying hours, and would be unable to fly again until they had been refuelled and serviced. But if 2 Para was to maintain contact with the rest of the battalion, a vital radio relay team was still required halfway between Goose Green and Fitzroy. Fortunately, just before last light, Brigadier Wilson flew in to Goose Green and was persuaded to loan his own helicopter for the task. This left him stranded at Goose Green for the evening, since his helicopter was also short of fuel, having only sufficient to drop off the relay team, under Corporal Banks, high up in the hills between the settlements.

LFFI had not yet given approval for the new plan. That night the Brigadier composed a long message, explaining the advantages of the proposed move over the original scheme.

---

* At this time there was only one Chinook helicopter for the entire force, the remaining three having gone down with the *Atlantic Conveyor* when she was struck by an Exocet guided missile on 25 May.

Meanwhile the acting CO had been joined at Goose Green by 'H' Jones's replacement, Lieutenant-Colonel David Chaundler, who had been flown out from the UK as soon as the news of Jones's death had come through. Almost unnoticed by the battalion, he had now jumped on one of the helicopters going forward, to land at the Fitzroy landing-site marked by Lieutenant Colin Connor's Recce Platoon. Clearly it was hardly the time to begin to assume command, and thus control of the battalion's move remained with Chris Keeble. By the time all the men had landed, it was already dark.

After his splendid handling of the battalion at Goose Green following the CO's death, his subsequent masterly negotiations with the Argentines for their surrender, and followed by the initiative displayed in launching the Fitzroy/Bluff Cove venture, Major Keeble might have been forgiven for thinking that he was just the man to be confirmed in command of 2 Para, at any rate until the end of the campaign.

Seconds-in-command exist, and are trained, to be able to take over a battalion when the CO is away for any reason, which may be for considerable periods. They are usually officers who have been recommended, and are fully qualified, to take over as a commanding officer. Moreover, during a battle, all concerned like to be led by someone they know and trust—'Better the devil you know than the one you don't.'

A second-in-command's is a most difficult appointment to fulfil to everyone's satisfaction. Most COs are inclined to be jealous of anyone who is able to usurp their authority in any way, and may therefore be reluctant to delegate more than is absolutely necessary. Thus the relationship between the two officers can be delicate. In addition, the CO is usually perfectly able to exercise command through his adjutant and other battalion staff with the result that, in the normal course of events, he may not be able to find much for his second-in-command to do. And when the CO is away, although he will have full responsibility, the second-in-command must continue to carry out the CO's policy in all matters, however much he may disagree with it. But once he has actually taken over command and begun to institute his own ideas, which may rectify and improve things where necessary, it can be agonising to have the authority removed without any apparent justification.

So for Major Keeble at this stage, it must have been a most testing experience to have to welcome and hand over command to another officer. For his part, his successor must have been fully aware of what might be passing through Keeble's mind; Colonel Chaundler had no alternative, however, other than to drop everything and fly out to join the battalion as soon as he possibly could.

Whether the decision to make the change came from the Ministry of Defence or whether it was a regimental requirement to stick to a seniority roster may never be known. With so few opportunities for officers to exercise command on active operations, the authorities may have felt that as Keeble had already proved himself so conclusively, it would be wrong not to let someone else do likewise. Whatever the reason, the two officers concerned were of such high calibre that there was not the slightest hitch, and the battalion's business was conducted as well as ever before.

At Fitzroy that night, Lieutenant Connor's Recce group had unfortunately been dropped off at the wrong location. Believing at the time that he had been correctly placed near the settlement, Connor had switched on his strobe-light to bring in the helicopters carrying the CO's party and the B Company group. Once landed, Major Keeble, assuming A Company to have landed correctly at Bluff Cove, ordered the Recce party to move to higher ground to establish communications, and this they did. But already the darkness had led to a loss of contact with the B Company group below, and Chris therefore decided that the best course would be to move forward to Fitzroy itself. Only then did the magnitude of the helicopter pilot's error become apparent, as the Paras realised that they were a full 4 kilometres short of the proposed landing-site.

The Recce patrols led off, followed by the CO's party, while the B Company elements remained on the ridge. Eventually Fitzroy came into view—a few houses, a large wool-shed down by the natural harbour, and a large bunk-house near the jetty. The first objective was the Manager's House in which Ron Binney lived, set at some distance from the hamlet in a hollow. Lieutenant Connor went forward with his radio operator: all was clear, and the rest of the force approached. Ron Binney soon produced tea and cakes for everyone, and told them that there were no Argentines in the settlement, but that attempts had been made by the enemy to blow the bridge on the track to Bluff Cove.

The Recce party was sent on in a civilian Landrover to inspect the damage. Arriving at the site, they could see detonation cords and seven or eight piles still prepared for demolition, as well as mines on the far side of the bridge—clearly a task for the Sappers. Of the piles, only one had been successfully destroyed, and thus the bridge could be made usable again. The patrol returned to Fitzroy with the good news.

The following day saw the arrival of more men from A, B, C and D Companies to join the advance parties at Fitzroy and Bluff Cove, C Company having now regained its company commander, Major Roger Jenner, who had discharged himself from the hospital at Ajax Bay hospital. The Brigadier had also flown forward and told Lieutenant-Colonel Chaundler, who had now assumed command of 2 Para, that he was going to move 5 Brigade Headquarters and its logistics to Fitzroy. The CO flew on to Bluff Cove to visit A Company, returning on foot to inspect the bridge, where Major Chris Davies of 9 Parachute Squadron, Royal Engineers, had already been at work with his men, lifting the mines. The guns of 29 Field Battery, RA were being positioned to provide artillery support for the battalion.

The overall plan was for B Company to hold the high ground dominating Fitzroy, A Company to hold the high ground immediately above Bluff Cove settlement with C Company in the offing to the north-east, and D Company to hold the high ground due east of Bluff Cove across the narrow mouth of the inlet. Battalion Headquarters was to be at Bluff Cove settlement itself, together with the RAP, both located in a local farm.

Ostensibly such a deployment would appear to create no major problems. In fact, to marry up the correct company to the correct locations became a major headache. Major Roger Jenner and C Company Headquarters found themselves dropped at Fitzroy instead of Bluff Cove; D Company was flown on to the east side of their hill in full view of enemy-held Mount Harriet, while the pilot searched for a landing-site; and there followed a shambolic move 2,000 metres up the hill whilst helicopters had to be hijacked to return piles of ammunition to the correct places because the landing-site had been wrongly marked.

Ominously, a 155-mm howitzer began to drop shells nearby, probably directed from Mount Harriet. D Company had become accustomed to 105-mm shelling during the Goose Green battle, but this was very different, exemplifying the sheer shock capability of the larger-calibre shell. It certainly spurred the company on.

It was as well that the C Company Headquarters party had indeed been landed at Fitzroy, for only from this position could the relay team, 25 kilometres away on the mountainside, be contacted on the radio, and thus a lengthy series of repetitions were required for any message to be passed from Bluff Cove to Goose Green. Corporal Banks's radio relay team was to have a hard time. High up on the hillside, completely isolated apart from four men of the Defence Platoon to give local protection, this small group provided the only link between the battalion and 'A' Echelon, now located at Goose Green. The team were to remain there for the next four days, cold, hungry, and soon soaked to the skin. Even when they were no longer vital to the move, they could not be evacuated because of low cloud and driving rain that had set in. This situation was not improved by fate: Corporal Banks's appendix chose this moment to 'grumble', although fortunately he had been replaced by Private Steve Bone, before the bad weather set in. But that was not all. Unknown to the relay team, a Gurkha patrol from Goose Green had decided that they were enemy, and a Harrier strike had been called in. Luckily the Command Post at Bluff Cove heard of the intended operation and was able to avert disaster.

The battalion gradually dug in on the new positions. Now that 3 Commando Brigade was firmly established on Mount Kent to the north an inter-brigade boundary was defined between 3 and 5 Brigades, with 2 Para being the nearest unit to 3 Brigade. There were problems of co-ordination, however, since areas such as Mount Harriet were visible to both brigades.

From their vantage point on the hillside, the men of D Company noticed some lights up on the high ground some way off to their left, on the lower slopes of Mount Harriet. They tried to engage with their mortars, but the range was too great. A day later, when artillery support was available, they adjusted their aim to a target area in the distance. That night they noticed, in the gap between Mount Challenger and Mount Harriet, a number of vehicles and troops. They called for gun fire, but the call was refused. They checked to ensure that the target was not friendly and called again, but were still refused since a shoot would involve firing across the inter-brigade boundary. That night more lights were seen, but again engagement was forbidden. The frustration of not being able to harrass the enemy, coupled with the steady rain that was now falling, was thoroughly demoralising.

Life had its moments, however. Early in the morning on the day after the battalion's arrival at Fitzroy, one of the locals approached C Company Headquarters. He stood talking for some time in general conversation and then made as if to go.

'By the way', he said, 'we've just had a telephone call from Island Harbour House. Some Argentine troops there have just stolen a Landrover and they're heading this way.'

'How long ago was this?' enquired Peter Kennedy, the company second-in-command.

'Oh, about an hour or two ago.'

'How long does it take to drive from there to here?'

'Oh, an hour or so.'

Island Harbour lies about 10 kilometres west of Fitzroy, slightly to the south. Lieutenant Kennedy organised an immediate ambush on the more likely approach to the settlement, and the civilian agreed to go with the ambush party, himself, suggesting the best site from which to intercept the vehicle.

They waited for two hours. It seemed that perhaps the Landrover was not coming after all, and Kennedy had just decided to move his men back to the settlement when, suddenly, there was the Landrover, coming round a corner with a white flag flying. The three enemy soldiers, an OP now quite far removed from its main body, surrendered gladly and were soon being questioned by Captain Alan Coulson, the Intelligence Officer.

Coulson's methods of getting information were subtle. First of all he took one of the men out to a hedge and sat staring him in the face for some fifteen minutes, saying nothing at all. His own features were somewhat stark: dark, intense eyes, a moustache, and a Mediterranean complexion had earned him the nickname 'Dago'. His expertise in 'fazing' people out was well known, almost Celinist.

The prisoner was then curtly told by the IO that his colleagues had already been interrogated, and had not only admitted that they both spoke perfect English, but had also already given away all the information that was needed. By this, the oldest trick in the book, the prisoner opened up, giving information about another observation post to the west of Goose Green. The information was quickly acted on, and later the Gurkhas made a successful capture.

At Bluff Cove a similarly amusing encounter arose at Battalion Headquarters. A tallish officer from another unit entered the barn that served as the Command Post—'Is this G Ops?' he asked. Images of a vast Divisional Headquarters sprang to mind. In the barn was 'G Ops': a map, a torch and two radios. 'These men? Is this all?' the officer continued, incredulously. The entire headquarters collapsed, giggling happily.

Battalion Headquarters was exceptionally well hosted. The farmstead belonged to Kevin and Diana Kilmartin, and had never been so much imposed upon by the Argentines as it was now by 2 Para, yet they rose to the occasion magnificently. Each day Kevin could be seen stomping around his farm, fair hair and beard blowing in the wind as he set about organising the slaughter of '365'—mutton—for the battalion's consumption. In the house Diana, a trained nurse, provided Captain Hughes's RAP with everything they asked for, virtually leaving them the whole ground floor.

Some of the 'local' inhabitants of Bluff Cove were as much strangers to the Falklands as were 2 Para. These were Poles, who had defected from a fishing vessel in February and had sought asylum in Port Stanley, moving on to Bluff Cove when the Argentines arrived. The battalion owed much to all the people of Fitzroy and Bluff Cove, and the one fear was that they might soon outstay their welcome. As a result, tight controls were placed upon all military personnel in the area to ensure that the locals were able to lead as normal a life as possible. Sadly, certain other visitors to Bluff Cove were later less circumspect in respecting the rights of those they had come to liberate.

As the battalion was settling in, 5 Infantry Brigade was slowly readjusting from its intended move from Sussex Mountain to Goose Green to its new destination at Fitzroy. The move was complicated, owing to the shortage and diversity of all types of transport, especially helicopters, which restricted the brigade to a gradual shuttle rather than a sudden swift deployment. Nevertheless, from the battalion's point of view information as to enemy or British dispositions was rarely forthcoming, as was any briefing on intended future plans. Probably as a result of the same lack of helicopters, visits by Brigade staff officers were rare, although the Brigadier came daily to discuss and help solve the various problems that confronted the battalion. 5 Brigade had literally been thrown together in the UK when 2 Para left for the Falklands, and it can take just as long for a brigade headquarters to find its feet as it can for any much larger unit.

Major Davies and his 9 Parachute Squadron, RE, had been busy for some days. The battalion's Assault Pioneer Platoon had already been trying to re-open the bridge from Bluff Cove to Fitzroy, removing demolition charges and repairing damage, and the additional expertise of the Sappers of 9 Squadron would ensure the rapid completion of the task. In the meantime, however, the movement of rations and other stores involved a precarious journey, in buffeting wind, across the damaged bridge's girders, reminiscent of the high parallel bars used on the confidence course back in Aldershot. Since no vehicles could yet be moved by this route, the local people would telephone each other in the two settlements and arrange for tractors to arrive at the bridge simultaneously. Stores would be handed over from one side to the other, and then taken up on the tractors.

By now the new CO had found the time to go round all the companies to introduce himself. His own introduction to the Falklands was nothing if not spectacular. Not many days before he had been in the Ministry of Defence, dealing with intelligence associated with the Falklands. One morning, as he and two other lieutenant-colonels from the Parachute Regiment, Mike Jackson and Peter Morton, left the Ministry building, having just heard of the death of Colonel 'H', Peter Morton had drily remarked that they had better pack their bags, since one or the other would probably soon be on the way. And David Chaundler it was to be.

His flight by VC10 to Ascension Islands and the subsequent fourteen-hour flight in a C-130 Hercules transport seemed to typify the entire operation: nothing was impossible, and if a new CO was required in the Falklands, then so be it. The C-130 had to be refuelled twice en route to its rendezvous with HMS

Penelope 100 miles north-east of the Falklands. Since the pilot had never before carried out an in-flight refuelling, there was always the possibility of this being a one-way trip for him as well as for 2 Para's new commanding officer.

The CO, after a long, uncomfortable flight, parachuted into the cold, grey Atlantic waters from 800 feet, and was soon aboard ship. A one-hour trip by Sea King to HMS *Hermes* for a 30-minute briefing by Rear-Admiral Sandy Woodward was followed by another two-and-a-half hour Sea King flight to HMS *Fearless* to meet Major-General Moore and Brigadier Wilson. Not many hours later he flew in to join 2 Para at Goose Green.

The new CO's style of leadership soon impressed itself upon the battalion. He was able to make a good start by conveying the admiration of everyone in the UK for what had happened at Goose Green, and by reading out the text of the Chief of the General Staff's signal of gratitude and congratulation.*

Colonel Chaundler went on to express a determination never to commit the battalion to an action without adequate fire support. Perhaps this aspect of battle was partly lost on most of the soldiers. Indeed, few of the officers either had begun to realise the potential for disaster at Goose Green, where fire support had often been ineffective, sometimes non-existent, and occasionally refused; since only one or two—Major Mike Ryan, for example—had in other campaigns experienced the full benefits of supporting arms, the officers were not yet fully aware of the difference supporting fire can make to a battle.

One of the CO's most noticeable changes was the holding, daily, of full 'O' Groups. Such meetings may appear irrelevant, time-wasting or unnecessary, but they had a considerable value in ensuring that the officers were aware, in advance, of all developments.

From his earlier intelligence briefings, the CO knew that the Argentines were highly unlikely to attempt a counter-attack. At the same time, however, he knew that sooner or later the final push to Stanley was bound to go ahead. For him, therefore, the real short-term need was to conserve the battalion, ensure that all men had the maximum amount of rest, and build up stores, so that everything would be ready and operating smoothly when the

---

* Reproduced in Appendix VI

time came. One result was that the Medical Officer was tasked to carry out a campaign of pre-emptive health care, touring the dug-outs looking for any soldier whose feet seemed in danger of causing problems later on. In all, thirty 'casualties' were eventually brought in, of whom twenty-eight were subsequently able to rejoin their companies for the final battle. The soundness of this policy is worth noting, for if a man was sent back to Ajax Bay for treatment, the chances of using him again were very remote.

The weather deteriorated markedly. High winds and rain lashed the men on the hillside, who could obtain only limited shelter from the peat walls they had constructed around their dug-outs. By now rations were again short and it was taking two to three days to ferry bergens forward from Goose Green. To add to the general mayhem, leading elements of the 2nd Battalion, the Scots Guards were due ashore at Bluff Cove on the night of 5/6 June, to take up positions forward of the battalion. Bearded SBS men had already reconnoitred the beach and pronounced it free from mines. The plot was for the Scots Guards and the 1st Battalion, the Welsh Guards to be the forward element of the Brigade, while 2 Para became the reserve battalion, remaining at Bluff Cove. In addition, most of the 1/7th Gurkha Rifles now in Goose Green would move up to give the brigade a strength of just under four battalions.

By the time they landed, on a foul night, the Scots Guards had had a thoroughly unpleasant time. After landing at San Carlos on 2 June, they had initially been sent up on to Sussex Mountain to occupy the old 2 Para positions, only to be told to march back down the hill again to be taken by the LPD HMS *Intrepid* on a long overnight voyage round to Bluff Cove. The journey by LCU from *Intrepid* to the landing-site had, in that weather, taken seven hours, and by all accounts had been horrendous, with green Atlantic waves shipping right over the men crowded on to the open decks. At one point the landing-craft had been shelled by a British frigate, which was only stopped by some frantic work on an Aldis lamp.

It was Lieutenant Peter Kennedy's task to go down to the landing-site to welcome these luckless men ashore. In the early morning of Sunday, 6 June the LCUs appeared and the ramps went down. A cultivated voice was heard from the leading craft:

'Are you Marines?'

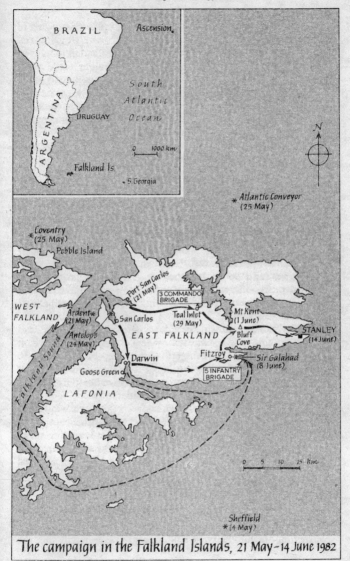

The campaign in the Falkland Islands, 21 May–14 June 1982

'No,' replied Peter.

'Are you 3 Para?'

'No,' again. 'We're 2 Para. Welcome to the Falklands.'

'Good God. Are you still here? We all thought you'd gone home after your battle. Don't we go home after battles here?'

The exhausted Guardsmen came ashore, each with a black dustbin-liner wrapped around him up to the waist. A spectator could not help comparing them now with their immaculate appearance when doing London duties.

In a single line their battalion moved through the pouring rain from the beach, over a ridge and down to Bluff Cove settlement. It was an unfortunate introduction to the campaign: soaked to the skin, cold, tired, and with many men nearly in a state of exposure after their long night, the Guards were in no shape to move directly into the field, as had been planned. Their operations officer arrived at Battalion Headquarters, 2 Para, asking whether anyone knew of the intended deployment of his battalion. Colonel Chaundler explained. A delay ensued until Lieutenant-Colonel Michael Scott, CO of the Scots Guards, arrived, well armed with an M-79 launcher. The Guardsmen waited patiently in the rain. By now several of them were suffering from exposure, and had to be brought into Kevin Kilmartin's house.

Clearly a major readjustment was necessary. Considering the amount of shelter available at Fitzroy, Colonel Chaundler suggested that since 2 Para was in any case the Brigade reserve, it would be advantageous if the battalion moved back to Fitzroy, leaving the accommodation at Bluff Cove to the Guards. The CO of the Scots Guards readily agreed, as did Brigadier Wilson when he arrived to meet the battalion commanders.

The weather was atrocious, with low cloud, high winds and driving rain, which precluded the use of support helicopters for the move. It was thought that the LCUs were still waiting at the mouth of the cove just over the ridge from the settlement, but their radios were switched off so this could not be confirmed immediately. Major Keeble took off in a light helicopter to persuade the LCU crews to help the battalion to move by the shortest route of all—by sea, direct to Fitzroy.

Unfortunately, by the time the helicopter was airborne the LCUs had moved off. A chase ensued, which ended in a haranguing match between the second-in-command and the

116

coxswain. Chris Keeble was a past-master at such negotiations. His style of bluff and rhetoric, matched by the occasional wave of his pistol in the coxswain's direction, soon left no doubt as to the urgency of the need. By late afternoon on 6 June the LCUs were once more at the mouth of the inlet east of Bluff Cove settlement, ready to take off D Company from the far bank and A and C Companies and Battalion HQ from the near side, B Company being at Fitzroy already. Eventually the battalion was embarked and ready to be moved across the 7 kilometres of water. The craft set off, with the men huddled beneath their waterproofs.

Land was sighted after some time afloat. It bore, however, no resemblance at all to Fitzroy—indeed, it looked remarkably familiar. Not surprisingly, for it was Bluff Cove, and the LCUs had beached again precisely where they had set off from three hours before, having completed a large circle.

In the CO's craft a very young Marine was sent out of the stern bridge to placate the Colonel.

'Why are we back at Bluff Cove?' the CO demanded.

'Well, sir, the radar's not working very well . . . and with all this kelp . . . the weather . . .'

'What you really mean is that you got f—— lost?'

'Well, yes sir.'

Hot soup appeared as a token of apology, and over in the D Company LCU some were even luckier, a bottle of rum helping to boost morale. Clearly navigation was not the crew's strong point. Captain David Constance, the Royal Marine liaison officer, winced.

They all set off again, the 'green' shipping over the side, or in some cases through holes into the well of the craft. The RSM was crouched beside the second-in-command. Major Keeble's fetish for Bounty bars was well known and, sure enough, there was still a box of 240 on board. The box burst open. Quietly the RSM expropriated and redistributed the booty. Munching a Bounty in such circumstances could hardly have been in the mind of the makers but it would make a good advertisement for their product.

This time the CO took a much closer interest in the navigation of the fleet, and as a fine dawn came up the jetty at Fitzroy came into view. Cold, wet and hungry, the men of 2 Para deposited themselves in the large wool-shed and its nearby bunk-house by the shore to dry out. Major Mike Ryan, in charge of 'A' Echelon, had thoughtfully laid on soup and a hot meal. At last the battalion was all together again.

It was during this morning that two unnecessary and almost tragic incidents occurred, almost within minutes of each other. In the wool-shed a soldier accidentally fired his weapon, fortunately without damage, and at almost the same time a signaller in the bunk-house did the same, a bullet from his submachine-gun hitting one of the Gunner party and seriously wounding him.

Probably the combined effects of the long night on the LCU followed by the relative relaxation of dry land and a warm, sunny day had induced a certain carelessness: whatever the reason, lethargy had nearly fatal consequences.

In situations such as these there is little that can be done, either as punishment or as prevention. The offending soldier knows that he has failed himself and his companions in an unacceptable manner, and for him there can be no more pronounced humiliation than the knowledge that his comrades will henceforth think twice before trusting him again. And it is trust—only trust—in each others' competence with weapons that is the basis for efficiency. It is fortunate that these two incidents did not occur in worse circumstances: had, for example, the submachine-gun been placed on automatic fire, the results in a confined space could have been horrendous. As it is, the penalty of suffering the acrimony, or contempt, of one's fellow soldiers can be felt twice as badly as any imposed punishment for offences of this nature. Yet even so, and correctly, both men were later charged in the normal manner for their breach of discipline. Being at war made no difference.

The battalion sorted itself out after the ordeal of the days on the hillside around Bluff Cove. By now B Company had been rotating a platoon at a time up on the ridge above Fitzroy, leaving the other two to dry out as best they could in Fitzroy settlement, aided by one of the locals, Ben Fanford, who had provided vehicles, food and other comforts. A and D Companies were allocated defensive areas to go to when required, and Battalion HQ was set up in the large bunk-house near the wool-shed. Meanwhile elements that made up 5 Infantry Brigade Tactical HQ were gradually arriving by helicopter from Goose Green, and had set up their operations in the large shed opposite the wool-shed. 'A' Echelon was also now in position in Fitzroy, having moved a considerable amount of stores and ammunition from Goose Green on a requisitioned civilian ship, MV *Monsunen*, an elderly coaster. And on the night of 6 June, two companies of Welsh Guards had been put ashore at Bluff Cove, although it had not been possible to land the remainder of the battalion, which had returned to Goose Green.

But administrative support for 2 Para was strained owing to the shortage of helicopters, which limited the supply of basic necessities. Communications to 'B' Echelon at Ajax Bay had now failed, despite all attempts made by the signallers, and consignments were therefore made on a hit-and-miss basis, with the result that much of the material intended for 2 Para almost certainly went to Brigade instead. Once again this showed up the need for helicopter marshalling teams to be attached to each forward battalion, equipped with landing-site identification markers designated for each unit.

'B' Echelon had by now been ashore for a considerable time. It too was facing problems, and the shortcomings of some peacetime logistical arrangements were fast becoming apparent. For example, the 'MFO' boxes, used to store all the battalion's equipment, proved to be hopelessly flimsy, quite unable to withstand the rigours of helicopter loading and of the prevailing weather conditions. Similarly, no thought had been given to how the Regimental PRI was to function in the long term. Soldiers need such items as cigarettes, razor blades and soap (which they have to buy for themselves) as much in the field as they do anywhere else. Unfortunately, the battalion's PRI was back in England, and so the Paymaster had to become a NAAFI stores controller in addition to his other duties. Besides this, many Task Force units that had come ashore were inadequately provided for. Some, for instance, had no means of charging radio batteries, and 'B' Echelon had to lend out cooking equipment and tentage. Unit quartermasters made exchanges based on mutual sympathy for each other's plight.

Meanwhile plans for the assault on Port Stanley were being finalised. The initial concept was for 3 Commando Brigade, now established on the west slopes of Mount Kent and on Mount Estancia to the north, to advance from the north-west to take Mount Longdon, Two Sisters and Mount Harriet, while 5

Infantry Brigade, consisting of the Welsh and Scots Guards, 1/7th Gurkhas and 2 Para in reserve, was to attack from the south-west, taking Mount William, Tumbledown and Sapper Hill.

Within 2 Para, it seemed that Sapper Hill might be a likely task for them as reserve battalion. Whilst the business of stocking up rations and ammunition was going on, commanders busied themselves in map study, and the IO made a large sand model in the bunk-house to help detailed planning.

Although there was a prevailing feeling of confidence, this was tempered with some reservations. Certainly a large number of Argentines had been defeated at Goose Green with relative ease, but the next offensive was to be against their best professionals—Marine and parachute units backed by a further seven regiments, each equivalent to a British battalion. In other words, a British force of seven battalions in total was to attack an enemy of greater strength in prepared positions on high ground. The Argentines had shown that they were capable of staunch resistance when properly led.

The realisation that Argentine C-130 Hercules aircraft were still unloading supplies every night at Port Stanley airfield was also very worrying. When D Company had reported this activity at Stanley, it was suggested that perhaps the sounds the company could hear were from our own ships at sea! The lack of activity by Argentine aircraft—the battalion had seen not a single A-4 Skyhawk, Mirage or Pucara since the battle for Goose Green, and attacks on the shipping in San Carlos Water had also diminished greatly—led to the conclusion that the Argentine air threat was no longer as great as it had been. A feeling of false security began to pervade the Task Force.

For 2 Para, the imminence of battle lent a real sense of purpose to the final preparation and the planning. In the CO's view, the days at Fitzroy were vital to the future success of the battalion, since a period of self-analysis allowed some of the shortcomings which had become apparent at Goose Green to be rectified. In particular, a thirty-five-man platoon was formed and earmarked purely for ammunition re-supply and stretcher-bearing in action, and a separate radio net for command and administration was also put into operation.

The movement of 'B' Echelon to Fitzroy had now got under way. A small advance party under the Education Officer,

Captain Mike Beaumont, had boarded the LSL *Sir Tristram* at Port San Carlos on Saturday, 5 June, from the *Norland*. Their main purpose was to take forward three days' rations for the battalion at Fitzroy. The sailing, due to leave early on Saturday morning, was delayed, and eventually the ship arrived at Fitzroy at first light on Monday the 7th. There were only six men from 2 Para on board, together with some seventy men from 5 Infantry Brigade. The Chief Officer of *Sir Tristram* was keen to get stores and ammunition off first, and only at the request of the troops were the 2 Para and Brigade parties put ashore. There were but two Bofors guns on board for AA defence, and from the ship the 2 Para party could see no air defences on the surrounding harbour, although the Blowpipe detachments were in fact in position. Beaumont's main concern was an enemy air attack, and he was glad to find himself and his men on land once more.

That night, *Sir Tristram* remained at Fitzroy. Before dawn on Tuesday, 8 June, some of B Company, up on the ridge above the settlement, noticed another ship coming slowly into harbour. This was the LSL *Sir Galahad*, carrying two companies of Welsh Guards that had been forced to return to Goose Green on the 6th, its Mortar Platoon and other battalion troops, together with the medical teams of 16 Field Ambulance. To the Paras' surprise, both ships remained at anchor. An LCU began unloading stores from the vessels, but no men were put ashore.

It was a lovely bright, clear day, for once, and the 2 Para companies took turns to move across the jetty to the spit of land that forms the cove on which Fitzroy sits, in order to zero their weapons on a makeshift rifle-range. Some men, their tasks complete, tried their hands at fishing with improvised rods.

C Company was the last to fire. At 1710 hours Lieutenant Kennedy gave the normal series of orders to the Recce Platoon as they lay prone, as if back on a gallery range in Aldershot: 'Five rounds, in your own time . . .' Suddenly he shouted: 'HALF RIGHT, RAPID FIRE!'

His voice was drowned by the roar of four Argentine A-4 Skyhawks as they flew in very low, dropping bombs over the ridge into the outer harbour.

There was pandemonium. The Blowpipe detachment's missiles flew harmlessly away, unable to catch the fast-moving jets from the side. Few men in the battalion had been aware that the two ships were in the harbour, and now everyone went flat in expectation of more bombs to come. Though none came, the buildings in Fitzroy were evacuated.

Outside, over the small ridge separating the inner and outer harbours, the two ships could be seen burning fiercely. The enemy aircraft had scored direct hits. The ship nearest the jetty, *Sir Tristram*, had been struck on the stern deck, and, although on fire, seemed otherwise to be safe, but the mortally stricken *Sir Galahad* could only be identified by the huge pall of black smoke that hung over her in the clear, still air.

All available helicopters in the area were immediately ordered to the rescue, and worked ceaselessly to bring casualties off the ships to the battalion's Aid Post. The pilots performed prodigies, landing on the ships' helicopter decks when they could, even though they were in constant danger from sudden explosions of ammunition or fuel on board, and at times, using the draught from their machines' rotors to 'fan' lifeboats and rafts away from the burning LSLs.

Lifeboats were launched by both ships, those from *Sir Tristram* going immediately to the aid of the much harder-hit *Sir Galahad*, and many men were able to reach safety by rowing ashore, often towing the liferafts with them. Medics ran down to the jetty to give help where they could, for a great number of the wounded were in a pathetic state, shocked, burnt, maimed and bleeding. Captain Hughes cleared the RAP of minor casualties, borrowing a phrase more apt had it come from the Padre; 'Take up thy beds and walk.'

For many of 5 Brigade's officers and men in Fitzroy, this was their first experience of war. On the beach, those of 2 Para who were immediately available waded into the sea, with others, to help to bring in some of the worst cases, while the RSM arranged guides to take the walking wounded to the RAP, many of whom were treated by men of the battalion. The elementary first-aid training they had all received paid dividends now.

As soon as casualties were able to be moved to the main hospital at Ajax Bay, they were passed on to Padre David Cooper, who was organising helicopter evacuation. The Brigade medical teams of 16 Field Ambulance had lost one officer and three men killed, and thirteen wounded, in the attack, and were in any case virtually non-operational now, having lost all their major equipment on the ship. 2 Para's RAP was now the Brigade Casualty Station in all but name, and Captain Rory Wagon once more came forward from Ajax Bay to assist the battalion.

Fitzroy Harbour was in full view of the enemy position on Mount Harriet, some 15 kilometres away; any observer on this hill with a good pair of binoculars could not have failed to see the two ships at anchor beyond the settlement. It is difficult, therefore, to remain detached about the disaster that occurred, since it was undeniably avoidable. By this time HQ 5 Brigade had three major units in and around Fitzroy and Bluff Cove—2 Para, 2nd Scots Guards, and most of 1st Welsh Guards—and in consequence it should have been functioning at full blast, fully aware of the disposition of all its troops, including those in transit, and prepared for any eventuality. There will always be calamities of this sort in wartime, but if they are due in the main to the shortcomings of a headquarters, then the event should be remembered, blame apportioned, and efforts made to see that they do not recur.

In fact, it seems that a series of factors, some of them unrelated, contributed to the disaster. First, embarkation of the troops at Ajax Bay on the previous night had been delayed, so that *Sir Galahad* did not arrive at Fitzroy until it was almost light. Second, those who planned the move thought that Rapier radar-guided missile batteries were available at Fitzroy to provide anti-air protection, whereas in fact the system was not yet functioning due to problems developed during transit. Additionally, a Harrier CAP had been in the air over Fitzroy only a short time before the attack, but had been called away to intercept another enemy raid. Third, the decision to unload ammunition and stores, including medical stores, before the soldiers, who could have been disembarked in a fraction of the time it takes to offload such material, was an appalling error of judgement, and one exacerbated by the fact that the Welsh Guards needed to join their main body at Bluff Cove, while 16 Field Ambulance was to disembark at Fitzroy. Given the damaged bridge, the swiftest way to Bluff Cove was by sea, so the Guardsmen remained on board. Fourth, HQ 5 Brigade was not aware that *Sir Galahad* was due that morning, and was therefore as surprised as B Company's soldiers to see the LSL glide into the harbour, since it was assumed that because she had not arrived at night, as planned, then her sailing must have been postponed to bring her in the following night. Even so, communication between the ship and 5 Brigade was virtually non-existent. And fifth, no air-raid warning reached *Sir Galahad*.

The combined effect of all these factors was that two entire companies of the Welsh Guards, with many other personnel, were still on board *Sir Galahad*, most of them in the ship's cafeteria or watching films on the open well-deck, when the bombing run took place. They had been at Fitzroy, in daylight, for some five hours, aboard a vessel carrying quantities of ammunition and fuel, and with inadequate defences against air attack. In all, thirty-six Welsh Guardsmen had been killed and many more wounded, of whom two died later, and eighteen other soldiers and sailors died, with others wounded. A valuable ship had been lost, and a fine battalion had suffered a shattering blow even before its campaign had begun, although its subsequent performance in battle was in no way impaired.

The enemy air attack had been carefully planned. A number of Argentine aircraft had been reported flying towards West Falkland as if to attack Ajax Bay, and a little before 1330 had bombed and severely damaged the frigate HMS *Plymouth*. All available Harriers, which only that morning had been on patrol over Fitzroy, had been scrambled to intercept, upon which the four enemy Skyhawks had approached Fitzroy, now virtually undefended against air attack, from an entirely different direction.

An hour later a second wave of aircraft came in, this time making for the settlement itself. They were met by the concentrated machine-gun fire of the whole battalion, and by fire from the Scots Guards. The leading aircraft was shot down and the remainder turned away. Far to the south-west another was seen to explode in mid-air, probably hit by a Sea Dart missile from a destroyer on the horizon. There was a second air raid some time later, equally ineffective, although one A-4, flying on from Fitzroy, succeeded in sinking an LCU making its way up from Goose Green with 5 Brigade vehicles aboard, causing further casualties. 8 June had been a bad day for the newly landed brigade, although Harriers caught some of the returning enemy aircraft and destroyed four.

The tragedy suffered by the Welsh Guards tended to cloak the good fortune of others. For within the wool-shed alongside the jetty during the first attack on the ships, a large and relatively easy target, there were large numbers of the battalion, still attempting to dry out and rest. Almost next door were the complete logistics and headquarters elements of 5 Infantry Brigade—bombs in either or both sheds would have turned a tragedy into a catastrophe.

Since a further attack on the wool-shed was still distinctly possible, the CO moved Battalion HQ further inland to Ron Binney's large house. Similarly, he ordered that the companies were all to be dispersed during daylight hours, returning to the wool-shed only at night for warmth and shelter.

When Brigadier Wilson visited that night, he stated that the Argentine air attack had considerably affected his plans, but that in any case it had now been decided that 2 Para would revert to 3 Commando Brigade. 'You will like 3 Commando Brigade,' Chris Keeble remarked to the CO. When Colonel Chaundler flew up to 3 Brigade HQ to be briefed, he was delighted with the way the 'O' Group was conducted. He found there a feeling of confidence rather different from that prevailing within 5 Brigade, which was still in the throes of reorganisation, and whose troops were, with the exception of 2 Para, as yet unused to the terrain and conditions, or to air attacks.

Following their CO's orders, 2 Para continued digging defences throughout the early hours of 9 June, in order to ensure complete cover by daybreak. The conifer trees around Ron Binney's house provided excellent cover from the air, and there was no shortage of defence stores, since corrugated iron from fences was commandeered for the purpose. The soldiers were determined not to be caught napping, and even David Norris of the *Daily Mail* showed himself to be a dab hand with a shovel after a short cadre on the intricacies of the two-man trench with overhead protection. Wednesday the 9th passed peacefully enough, however, although there was considerable speculation about and anticipation of the forthcoming move back under the command of 3 Commando Brigade.

Yet a threat still remained, and in the early hours of 10 June warning was received of a possible ground and air attack on Fitzroy. The civilians were warned and the battalion stood to all morning, but it proved to be a false alarm and nothing came of it.

On the following morning the CO and the company commanders flew on ahead to an OP on the shoulder of Mount Kent, to have a look at the routes the battalion might have to take. 2 Para was to have some formidable support, for by now a troop of Scorpions and Scimitars from the Blues and Royals had been placed under command on request. In addition, Captain Roger Field of the same regiment, who had been a watch-keeper in 5 Infantry Brigade Headquarters, managed to find an excuse to come along as a tank liaison officer, leaving the Education Officer, to his chagrin, to take his place. And Lieutenant C.R. Livingstone's Recce Troop from 59 Independent Commando Squadron, Royal Engineers, was back again, with additional Sapper support from Sergeant Cork's troop of 9 Parachute Squadron, RE.

Rations were again running short, and centralised cooking once more replaced the diet of dehydrated arctic food. Contrary to expectations, the centralised feeding was wholeheartedly disliked, and soldiers could be seen gazing longingly at the unopened packets of Chicken Supreme or Beef and Mutton that were to serve them in the days ahead. There could be little doubt where preferences lay.

The lift of the battalion later that day was an example of the efficient use of helicopters. Under the watchful eye of Captain David Constance, the Marine Liaison Officer with 2 Para, chalks were lined up as markers in the field next to Ron Binney's house as upwards of three or four Sea Kings began ferrying companies on the short journey to a lying-up position (LUP) to the west of Mount Kent. Each man collected four mortar bombs as he waited—there was to be no shortage of ammunition this time.

The concentrated use of helicopters allowed the battalion to be rapidly redeployed in the rear of 3 Commando Brigade, near the Headquarters, with the minimum of fuss or delay. By last light the move had been completed and the companies dispersed into their own areas. The weather was perfect, and the evening sun brought on a feeling almost of languor as men brewed up and relaxed. Below them and to the north-west could be seen the beautiful shimmer of the waters of Teal Inlet, and the chimneys of Estancia House peacefully disgorged spirals of peat smoke into the clear air.

By now the company commanders had rejoined the battalion from their recce, and as light faded the CO gave his orders for the move. 2 Para was going to battle once more.

CHAPTER 7

Wireless Ridge and Stanley

Night fell. Men zipped themselves into their sleeping-bags to rest before the next stage, due to start at midnight. The conditions were balmy, but time spent in idle thought or in sleep soon passes, and before long the bergens were being re-packed for the last time as each company moved forward to take its place in the dreaded 'Airborne snake'. The packs and sleeping-bags were dropped off at 'A' Echelon and, guided by the lights of the patrols of C Company, the long procession began.

The plan was for 2 Para to move up to an assembly area on a col to the north of Mount Kent, on the main track to Stanley. Here the battalion would wait while 3 Para and 45 Commando took Longdon and Two Sisters and while 42 Commando went on to take Harriet. It was the former two attacks that most concerned the battalion.

The column eventually moved off, with the usual and inevitable characteristics of any night move: stopping and starting, sitting down for brief respite and then having to increase the pace where gaps appeared in the chain, sweating under loads and then shivering as the wetness was felt on the back. Now stomach upsets began to take a toll. On either side of the line of the march, round white shapes could occasionally be seen poised above the icy ground, luminous in the moonlight like a number of belisha beacons, providing a series of markers along the route for others to follow. The smell revealed the true nature of this phenomenon, and there would be a scurrying as the unfortunate individual who had been caught short hurried

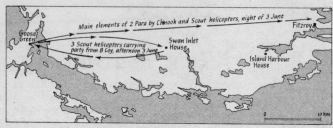

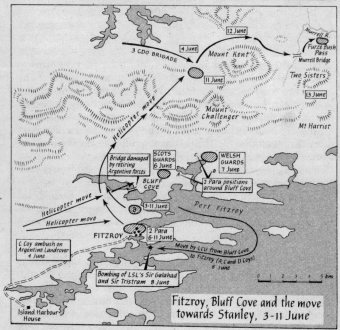

Fitzroy, Bluff Cove and the move towards Stanley, 3-11 June

to find his section again. That last meal in Fitzroy was taking effect.

The night and the march dragged on. There was the sound of battle from far off to the east as 3 Para and 45 Commando began their attacks on the well defended hill-tops, and occasionally red tracer could be seen arcing gently, silently, into the night sky. Gunner batteries, now behind the battalion, began shelling in support, and their rounds could be heard whirring overhead.

For some, it was a novel experience. Roger Field of the Blues and Royals was not at all used to having to walk with the 'grunts', as the 'lumpers' called the infantry. He plodded on, perhaps a little regretful at having been so hasty in chasing his new appointment. But if this was what adding a little tone to a brawl entailed*, then so be it, although his thoughts wandered to a large bottle of whisky left behind in his rucksack in the LUP.

Warm and sweating after so much exertion, the battalion at last reached its destination, just below the brow of the col between Mounts Kent and Estancia. On their right Mount Kent loomed large and black, and the companies moved into separate areas and waited. Brewing-up and smoking was allowed if carefully concealed—a risk, perhaps, but provided that the enemy had left no stay-behind parties it was well worth the boost to morale. Two patrols from the Recce Platoon were sent forward as a screen.

As Major Roger Jenner went around to check his men, he suddenly noticed a large tent and strangers within it. It proved to be the 45 Commando Regimental Aid Post. A Marine appeared, mentioning that he had been expecting 2 Para, although the battalion had not been expecting to see him.

Now that men were halted they soon began to feel the bitter cold. Some tried to sleep, putting on their bundled arctic padded trousers and their waterproofs, but even thus clad, the frozen earth gave no comfort as the sweat dried on their backs. It was an awful, long wait. Soon soldiers were marching up and down, practising foot drill in an endeavour to restore circulation to wet feet that were now near to freezing.

News was sparse but good. 3 Para and 45 Commando had both

---

* An old Army joke: a young cavalry officer, asked the purpose of cavalry on the field of battle, replied that it was 'To lend tone to what would otherwise be a vulgar brawl.'

taken their objectives, even though the latter had been two and a half hours late on the start-line after a difficult approach march. Little further was known about 2 Para's future role, for since the battalion was working on insecure radio, all directions had to be given in code. Eventually they received the order to move off again, and their destination, given in code, was deciphered and checked on the map. It needed considerable checking, for the new location was given as the top of Mount Kent! The mistake was eventually rectified, and the warning order to move forward again was passed down. Rarely had it been so well received, for the bitterly cold men would have gladly run the next two miles to get warm again.

The halt had not been without its lighter moments. The RMO, Captain Hughes, had developed a fixation that he would never live to see his twenty-sixth birthday. He was very wrong, however, and at 0200 on 12 June, the hour and day of his birth, he was greeted with a rousing chorus of 'Happy Birthday' from the Padre and 2nd Lieutenant Mark Coe.

It was now assumed, though it had not been clearly stated, that the battalion was to move in support of 3 Para. As the column moved down the slope from the col, it was obvious that a battle was still being fought on Mount Longdon. Occasionally a purposeful Gazelle would pass overhead, flying 'blind' to bring casualties back from the battle, and enemy shells were landing over to the left of the route, quite harmlessly. The column progressed, snaking to and fro to avoid the wettest parts of the boggy ground.

In the twilight of early morning Murrell Bridge, due north of Two Sisters, at last loomed into sight. A long halt ensued, while enemy shells burst to the front. The battalion was due to rendezvous here with 3 Para, and the CO was concerned that this link-up would now take place in broad daylight. Brigadier Thompson arrived, however, and reaffirmed the need to push on. But a minefield had been detected directly to the battalion's front and a change of direction was therefore necessary, forcing the battalion to pass through an area known to be registered as a target for Argentine defensive artillery fire.

Lower down the chain of command, few in 2 Para had any idea at all of what was happening, and this lack of information bred uncertainty. The change in direction was effected and the battalion turned north on a route which followed the contour above the river valley along the west side of the Mount Longdon feature. Enemy 155-mm shells continued to land to the left, to the right, in front or behind the column, and it was fortunate that none found their mark, for at times men were bunched up, and even one hit would have killed or wounded many. Apparent indifference to the shelling was noticeable among the veterans of Goose Green, who remained calm and cheerful throughout, although, not surprisingly, those who had not actually experienced the earlier battle showed rather less complacency.

As it grew lighter, the companies began to open out. The column turned east and moved onwards along the line of the Murrell River, with Mount Longdon on the right, now, since dawn, in the hands of 3 Para. Some of the more heavily laden soldiers, such as medics and signallers, were beginning to get tired, but it was to be another fine day and the cold of the night had long been forgotten.

Major John Crosland went forward to recce a steep-sided gully known as Furze Bush Pass, where a tributary joined the Murrell River. As an assembly area it proved to be an admirable choice, for although Argentine shelling had seemed to follow the battalion on its route, the nature of the rocky scarp effectively prevented any rounds from reaching the area. Now shellfire could only land either above the gully, on the lower slopes of Mount Longdon, or plunge harmlessly into the marshy area of the river itself, a good 200 metres away. Although at times the shells would air-burst, the fuses were never correctly set and they invariably exploded harmlessly high in the air.

In the gully, Crosland had found a party under Major Butler from the 3 Para Patrols Company. They described the battle for Longdon as best they could. Many gallant actions had been fought, including one in which Sergeant Ian McKay had cleared an enemy bunker with grenades under intense fire, only to be killed at the moment of his triumph. For this outstanding act Sergeant McKay was later awarded a posthumous Victoria Cross. Casualties in 2 Para's sister battalion had been relatively high, however, and were still being caused by the continuous artillery pounding they were taking, but the mountain had been taken and would be held.

As 2 Para moved into Furze Bush Pass the order to dig was

given. It was hardly needed, for the habit of digging was now so inbred that it was done automatically. In the soft peat a two-man shell scrape could be dug quickly enough for the results to provide a reasonable degree of protection from shelling, mortaring or aircraft attack.

But to some, digging was quite a novel experience. Captain Roger Field was introduced to the art, with moderate success. He later confessed to the CO, 'When I left Sandhurst, I swore I would never again march, dig a trench, or blacken my face, but within twenty-four hours you have managed to get me doing all three.' He had discovered that there is quite a considerable difference between living, eating and sleeping from a nice warm tank, and doing so with the 'grunts'.

That day—Saturday, 12 June—passed quietly, with clear skies and bright sunshine letting men doze comfortably among the rocks, and the fresh waters of a stream racing through the gully allowed ample brews of tea and coffee. As yet there were no plans for bergens to be brought forward from 'A' Echelon, back on Mount Kent, for everyone expected to have to launch an attack at last light. Later on, the CVR(T)s of the Blues and Royals arrived.

Far away to the east, an enemy Chinook and a Huey helicopter were observed landing in the area of a settlement on the marshy bank of the estuary. Artillery fire was called down and the helicopters quickly flew off, but, just as quickly, the guns had to stop, for one of the locals had used the civilian radio telephone to complain of being shelled!

For some time now the CO had been asking Brigade for orders, and at 1800 hours Major Hector Gullan arrived by helicopter. He ran over to Lieutenant-Colonel Chaundler, saying, 'It's Wireless Ridge tonight, Colonel.' The CO was far from pleased, for this must have been one of the shortest sets of orders for a battalion night attack ever given, and there was precious little time to take all the necessary measures. Nevertheless, a hurried 'O' Group was called and immediately got under way.

Wireless Ridge is a dual spur feature running off eastwards from Mount Longdon. The north-west spur is wide and covered on its flat, open summit by a series of peat ponds, while to the south lies Wireless Ridge proper—a narrow, rocky ridge-line running due east above Moody Brook to form the north side of Stanley harbour.

The enemy on the large spur to the north were believed to be administrative troops, possibly a regimental headquarters, but exactly what was on the southern ridge-line remained uncertain, although it was known to be defended. The CO's immediate plan was for the battalion to attack from the north, with A Company left, B Company right and D Company and the troop of Scorpion and Scimitar in reserve. C Company would secure the start-line, and a troop of Sappers would be available to deal with any minefields as and when they might be encountered. H-hour was provisionally set for just after midnight (0030), and the battalion was to have the support of one artillery battery at priority call.

The 'O' Group was almost over when Major Gullan suddenly interrupted as news came in from Brigade of a change in boundaries between assaulting units. The CO winced and re-examined his map to see how this would affect his plan.

Within a few minutes, however, he no longer had to worry. The attack was cancelled. The Gurkhas and Scots Guards were due that night to attack Mount Tumbledown and Mount William, and 42 Commando was to attack Mount Harriet, with the Welsh Guards, reinforced by two companies of 40 Commando to replace its missing companies, in reserve. It was not feasible for 2 Para to take its objective until the two former features had been secured, because Wireless Ridge was entirely dominated by Tumbledown, but the two assaulting battalions had not had the time, the ammunition or rations, or, in the end, the helicopter lift forward to be able to assault that night. Major-General Moore therefore reluctantly agreed with Brigadier Wilson that 5 Brigade's attack should be postponed for twenty-four hours, and so 2 Para's assault was of necessity put back. In a sense this was as well, since no time had been allowed for detailed reconnaissance of the enemy position on Wireless Ridge or for adjustment of targets, and the orders had necessarily been hurried.

Lieutenant-Colonel Chaundler flew to Brigade Headquarters to find out what was happening. Brigadier Thompson corrected the earlier order that the attack was cancelled—it was only postponed. Now at least aware of a definite target for the morrow, the CO returned and arrangements were made to bring forward from Mount Kent the battalion's mortars, machine-guns, additional ammunition, bergens and the secure radio trailer.

Now everyone settled down for a second night without sleeping-bags, only this time there would be no march to restore the circulation. There were some novel ideas for providing the best possible insulation in the shell-scrapes, and piles of heather were heaped into the dug-outs to provide comfort and warmth. Even then, as the long night wore on so the cold grew, and feet and toes soon became numb, like blocks of ice.

Yet, unbelievably, the Argentines could still be heard using the runway at Stanley—indeed it was now possible to see the runway lights and to watch as the C-130 Hercules transports landed after the long flight from Argentina. Unfortunately the airport was still just too far out of range to be shelled by British artillery.

It is interesting to reflect that these relatively slow and cumbersome transport aircraft were able to continue to operate in such circumstances. Given the sophisticated modern anti-aircraft resources available to the three services, as well as the bombing and naval bombardment of the airfield, one would have thought that the enemy's re-supply operations could have been brought to a complete halt, but in fact aircraft flew in to and out of Stanley throughout the campaign. One is tempted to wonder whether a massive air withdrawal (had sufficient transports been available) might not have presented the Argentines with a viable alternative to abject surrender. Among the men of 2 Para waiting to attack, however, such thoughts were rare, although there was dismay that the Navy and Air Force had failed to block a vital supply route, however difficult it might have been to do so.

There was no need to call for a stand-to as dawn approached. A voluntary drill parade took place as soldiers marched up and down, stamping their feet, some even holding miniature physical training sessions in their attempts to thaw out. Few had slept, except David Norris of the *Daily Mail*, who had proved the most cunning. All through the previous day he had tramped with the battalion, carrying a bag tied together with string in a most unmilitary manner. When night fell, however, he had pulled from that ungainly receptacle a beautiful arctic sleeping-bag, and despite bids for a quick sale he had slept soundly within it. With hindsight, the additional weight and bulk of the men's sleeping-bags would easily have been more than compensated for by the warmth and psychological benefit that a 'green maggot' brings.

At 1200 hours on Sunday, 13 June the 'O' Group assembled once more. The ground was described again in detail. On Wireless Ridge, towards it eastern end, was a line of telegraph poles running almost due south down to the old Moody Brook barracks, now ruined by shell-fire, where the former Royal Marine garrison of the Falklands had been housed before the invasion. West of the poles the ridge was neatly divided from north to south by a track, with a wider, 300-foot feature to its west and the narrower rocky ridge running away to the east, crossed by the telegraph wires some 800 metres along. A road from Stanley, also flanked by telegraph poles, ran past the barracks along the Moody Brook, petering out beneath Two Sisters to become the main track to Estancia House. A stream to the north of the larger and wider pond-covered spur was also noted.

More details of the enemy were given. The headquarters of the Argentine 7th Infantry Regiment was thought to be amongst the peat ponds on the northern spur, and there were believed to be troops in the Moody Brook area near the barracks, including part of an armoured car squadron. Elements of the Argentine 1st Parachute Regiment were thought to be in the area, and to the east, on the race-course on the outskirts of Stanley itself, were a number of 'Triple As', now well respected as anti-infantry weapons. Mines had been laid in various places.

The Scots Guards and Gurkhas would attack Tumbledown that night, and elements of D and G Squadrons, 22nd SAS, would meanwhile be on Wireless Ridge to the east of the telegraph wires, in order to create a diversionary attack. 3 Para's A Company was positioned on the lower slopes of Mount Longdon, east and slightly to the north of Wireless Ridge, with B Company of the same battalion actually on the summit, and C Company to the east of A by about 1,000 metres. Two batteries of guns, a Type 21 frigate, HMS *Ambuscade*, and the troop of Blues and Royals tanks were in support to 2 Para.

2 Para's task was to capture the Wireless Ridge features, keeping west of the telegraph wires, and Colonel Chaundler's plan called for a two-phase noisy night attack. In Phase 1, A

Company would take the northern spur where the ponds were, C Company having secured the start-line. Once this was secure Phase 2 would come into operation, and B and D Companies would pass through from the north to attack the main Wireless Ridge feature itself. B Company would go to the right (the western end of the ridge), while D Company attacked the rocky ridge-line east of the track.

The mortars would move forward from Mount Kent to a position in the lee of the hillside south of Drunken Rock Pass, and this would also be the site for a static Battalion Headquarters during the attack. H-hour was again to be at about 0030. The importance of digging in on the objectives was emphasised once more, since Wireless Ridge was dominated by both Tumbledown and Sapper Hill, and if enemy troops should still be there at dawn they could make 2 Para's positions untenable.

The orders were straightforward, and the plan simple, involving the maximum use of darkness. As the 'O' Group ended the company commanders were told that they would now fly up to Mount Longdon to look at the ground over which they would operate.

The CO went on ahead with the Battery Commander to meet Lieutenant-Colonel Hew Pike, CO of 3 Para, and Major William McCracken, RA, who controlled the artillery 'anchor' OP on Mount Longdon. They discussed and arranged for co-ordinated fire support, with 3 Para's mortars, Milan teams and machine-guns all ready to fire from the flank, and Major Martin Osborne's C Company, 3 Para, in reserve.

Back at the gully all was peaceful in the bright sunshine. Suddenly this was shattered as nine Skyhawks appeared further to the north, flying very low in formation and heading due west towards Mount Kent. The effect was electric, for no one expected that the Argentines could still flaunt their air power in this way.

At 'A' Echelon, behind Mount Kent, there was no doubt as to who the jets were aiming for. As they came screaming up over the col and rose to attacking height, the formation split: three went for the area where the artillery gun-line had recently been, three went for 3 Commando Brigade HQ, and three attacked 'A' Echelon. All the machine-guns opened up, claiming one possible hit as the bombs rained down. Amazingly, there were no casualties from this minor blitzkrieg. But the accuracy of the attack, and its obvious definiteness of purpose, left people wondering if the enemy had left concealed OPs behind, watching Mount Kent, or if satellite photography had shown up the various targets or, possibly, if Argentine electronic-warfare equipment had picked up radio signals from Brigade HQ.

The air raid created delays to all helicopter movement, but eventually the CO was able to fly on to Brigade HQ, while the company commanders were dropped on to Mount Longdon for their own recces. Colonel Chaundler had already been updated on the actual strength of the enemy, which was greater than had been thought, and a new Argentine position had been detected to the east of the pond-covered spur, on a knoll overlooking Hearnden Water and the mouth of the Murrell River.

While the CO was at Brigade HQ, the company commanders were able to study Wireless Ridge in detail from the commanding position on Longdon. It at once became obvious that much of the information so far given to them was inaccurate. What was thought to be C Company of 3 Para proved to be nothing of the sort: Major Dair Farrar-Hockley noticed that it was an *enemy* position of about company strength, situated dangerously on the flank of the 2 Para axis of attack, west of the northern spur. It was also clear that Wireless Ridge proper was heavily defended, with positions which stretched a long way to the east beyond the line of telegraph poles that marked the 2 Para boundary. Strangely, no harrassing fire was being brought to bear during the day on any of the Argentine positions, and their soldiers were free to stand about in the open.

The company commanders flew back to Furze Bush Pass, but clearly a major change in plan was necessary. The CO returned from Brigade HQ as evening approached and was told of the situation. 'Go away and have your supper. Come back in forty-five minutes and you will have a new set of orders,' he said. Meanwhile the move-up of mortars and the adjustment of artillery had been delayed, and as a result the changes to the fire-plan had to continue into the night, directed by the OP on Longdon and using illuminating rounds.

Unfortunately for the company commanders, normal battle procedure had already ensured that relevant details of the first plan had permeated to the lowest level. Platoon and section commanders had had time to issue clear and well constructed orders to their subordinates, but now their efforts were all useless, for by the time the company commanders returned with the CO's revised plan, it was too late to go into new details. Such a sudden last-minute change did little for the men's faith in the system, but it was unavoidable and, in any case, the soldiers had by now become stoical, while the cynics among them were not disappointed by this evidence of fallibility at higher levels. Nevertheless, the battalion was able to adapt and change its plans and moved off on time. But Phil Neame had his misgivings about what the SAS to the east of his line of advance was *meant* to be doing, and there was no knowledge of what the SAS was actually *going* to do. Furthermore, no one really knew what was beyond Wireless Ridge to the south, in the Moody Brook area, and everyone would have liked to have known exactly when the 5 Brigade attack on Tumbledown was timed to begin.

The battalion's new plan was for a four-phase noisy night attack. In Phase 1 D Company would capture the newly discovered enemy position west of the northern spur; A and B Companies would then assault the pond-covered hilltop; Phase 3 called for C Company to take the knoll to the east; and finally D Company would roll up the enemy on Wireless Ridge itself, with fire support from A and B Companies, starting in the west and finishing at the telegraph poles.

Fire support was to be lavish in comparison to Goose Green: two batteries of 105-mm guns, HMS *Ambuscade* with her one 4.5-inch gun offshore, and the mortars of both 2 and 3 Para, totalling sixteen tubes. Ammunition was plentiful, and the battalion's mortars had been moved complete from Mount Kent by helicopter, and were thus fresh for action. The Machine-Gun Platoon had also been flown forward. Between the six guns they had enough ammunition to provide a massive weight of fire, and the men were fresh and rather proud of their earlier achievement behind Mount Kent against the Skyhawks. The Milan Platoon was already forward with the battalion—the experience of Goose Green had demonstrated the capability of this precision guided missile against static defences. Finally the light tanks of the Blues and Royals would be there, Scimitars with their 30-mm automatic cannon and Scorpions with 76-mm guns, and both equipped with very high quality night-vision equipment and having superb cross-country performance. All available support was allotted first to D Company, then to A and B in their assault, and finally to D Company again as it traversed the ridge.

As night closed in the tanks, the mortars and the Recce Platoon, which was to secure the start-line, moved up. By now the promise of the day had vanished and snow and sleet were falling, considerably limiting the effectiveness of all the gun-sighting equipment, and reducing visibility.

At about 0015 a storm of fire from the supporting artillery and mortars was unleashed upon the Argentine positions. A and B Companies passed by, led by C Company patrols to the new start-line secured by Corporal Bishop's patrol in the relatively safe ground overlooking Lower Pass. At 0045 hours on Monday 14 June, D Company moved over its own start-line further to the west, and headed towards the identified enemy position.

As the company moved forward, the tanks of the Blues and Royals and the machine-guns provided fire support while the artillery increased its rate of fire. Enemy mortar fire in retaliation became heavy. In the rear of the company, Private Godfrey of 12 Platoon had a near miss as a piece of shrapnel cut through his windproof and dug into his boot. He dived for cover—straight into an Argentine latrine!

The weight of supporting artillery and mortar fire was singularly effective, for the enemy on the D Company objective could be seen running away as the company pushed forward, although 155-mm air-burst shelling increased as the Paras began to clear the Argentine trenches, now-abandoned except for a few enemy killed by the barrage. The darkness of the night and the extent of the enemy position caused the company to spread out, creating problems of control. Lieutenant Webster of 10 Platoon counted up to twenty trenches on his right, with more over to the left, where 2nd Lieutenant Waddington's 11 Platoon found the other half of the assault formation.

Occasionally as they moved forward, men would suddenly disappear into the freezing water of an ice-covered pond. Privates Dean and Creasey of 11 Platoon went in up to their necks, and had to tread water to stay afloat until their platoon sergeant, Sergeant Light, dragged them out.

Fire support for the company was immaculate. The tanks used their powerful image-intensifier night-sights to pinpoint targets.

Once enemy positions were identified, they fired. As soon as the battalion's machine-gunners saw the strike they, too, opened up. Occasionally the machine-gun fire was too close for comfort, even for D Company, and in the end 10 Platoon Commander called for it to stop.

The opposition had fled, and D Company took its first objective in record time, remaining *in situ* while A and B Companies began their part of the battle. Enemy artillery fire was increasing, however, and Neame therefore decided to push forward for another 300 hundred metres into relative safety, to avoid the worst of the barrage.

Several of those waiting to move on the A and B Company start-lines were reminded of scenes they had seen from films of the First and Second World Wars. As shells landed all around, men lay huddled against the peat, with bayonets fixed. There could be no denying that, for the soldiers, fear of the known was in this case worse than blissful ignorance of the unknown. In the shelter of the peat bogs some smoked, watching the display of illuminants above.

Just as the time came to move, the shelling claimed its first victim, for Colour Sergeant 'Doc' Findlay was killed in the rear of A Company, and soldiers from Support and HQ Companies were also wounded. The advance began, the two companies moving southwards parallel to each other, on either side of the track. The men crossed the stream in the valley north of their objective with the tanks firing over their heads. The effect upon the enemy was devastating. In their night-sights the tank crews could see Argentine soldiers running or falling as the accurate fire took effect. The boost to morale that this form of suppressive fire gave was considerable; fundamentally, the battle was being won by supporting arms, the infantry being free to do their own job, which is actually clearing and securing the ground.

On the left, all was going well with A Company. Command and control had been well practised back at Goose Green and now the junior officers and section commanders were quite expert in maintaining direction. Silence was unnecessary and orders were shouted backwards and forwards. The enemy were still shelling as the companies advanced, but now counter-battery fire was being provided by our own artillery. From his own position the CO could see the two companies in extended formation, moving quickly up the hill, the whole battlefield brightly lit by starshell.

Co-ordinating the two assaulting companies' advances was difficult, however. The track provided a boundary of sorts, but controlling upwards of 200 men during a noisy battle over difficult terrain is not easy. Colonel Chaundler had another worry. Earlier, before the battalion had moved up, he had been shown a captured Argentine map which indicated a minefield directly in the path of the assaulting companies. There was only fifteen minutes to go before 2 Para set off—far too late for a change of plan. The CO only had time to brief OC B Company, while John Crosland had none in which to warn his men, and in any case was told to push on regardless, since there would be no time to clear the mines. Only afterwards did Major Crosland tell his men that they had actually moved directly through the minefield without knowing it. Miraculously, no one was blown up on the way.

The ponds on the spur claimed a victim, however, when Private Philpott of 5 Platoon suddenly plunged into over six feet of water. He was dragged out and his section commander, Corporal Curtis, immediately organised a complete change of clothing from the other men in the section, which probably saved Philpott's life.

The two companies consolidated on the objective. There was some firing from the trenches, swiftly silenced as the men of both companies ran in to clear them. Once more the enemy had fled, leaving only twenty or so of their number behind, quickly taken prisoner as they were winkled out of their holes. Radios were still switched on, and several dead lay around the positions. As the men dug in, the enemy shelling increased and it was to continue for the rest of the night at the same level of intensity. Most thought it was worse than Goose Green, but fortunately the abandoned enemy bunkers provided reasonable shelter, although a number of casualties occurred in A Company.

It was now C Company's turn. Already they had had a minor scare on the A and B Company start-line when a Scorpion tank had careered towards Company Headquarters in the darkness. It was hopelessly lost and its commander had to be evacuated after a dose of 'hatch rash'—the effect of placing the head in the path of a rapidly closing hatch. The confused vehicle was soon heading in the right direction, but now under the command of Captain Roger Field, who had seized this opportunity to revert to a more honourable role than foot-slogging.

With A and B Companies now firm, C Company was ordered to check out the Argentine position further to the east that had been spotted from Mount Longdon on the previous day. Major Roger Jenner was glad to be moving again, for it seemed that the supporting artillery battery had developed a 'rogue gun' and every sixth round meant for the enemy was coming in uncomfortably close to his company. He and his men set off, taking cover occasionally on the way as shells fell close by. There had been no firing from the company objective during the battle, and soon the platoons were pushing round the side of a minefield on to the knoll.

As the Recce Platoon advanced, they could hear noises of weapons being cocked. The bright moonlight left them uncomfortably exposed on the hillside. On the forward edge of the slope were two parallel lines of rock, and on the second line the platoon found a series of shell scrapes, suggesting recent occupation by a body of troops. Once again it seemed that the enemy had left hurriedly, leaving tents and bits of equipment behind in the process. Away over to the east Jenner's men could see the bright lights of Stanley airfield, and could hear a C-130 landing. The company was ordered to dig in, but since an enemy attack on this feature was extremely unlikely the CO changed the orders, and C Company moved up to the pond-covered hill.

If any particular group deserves special praise for what was done that night, then it must be the tanks of the Blues and Royals. Their mere presence had been a remarkable boost to morale during all the attacks that had taken place, and the speed and accuracy of their fire, matched by their ability to keep up with the advancing Paras, had been a severe shock to the enemy. Lance-Corporal Dunkeley's tank, which Captain Field had taken over following the injury to its commander, had alone fired forty rounds from its 76-mm gun.

2 Para was performing superbly, its three first objectives taken with great speed and a minimum of casualties, despite heavy and accurate enemy artillery fire. Whenever the enemy in trenches had sought to return fire they had been met by a withering concentration of fire from the rifle companies' weapons which,

coupled with very heavy support, had proved devastating. It is not known whether the Argentines had gathered that they were facing the men from Goose Green, but there can be no question that 2 Para knew.

D Company was now ready to go into the final phase of the attack and began moving forward again to the west end of Wireless Ridge. The tanks and support weapons moved up to join A and B Companies on the hilltop overlooking the D Company objective, and endured the artillery fire as well as anti-tank fire from Wireless Ridge to the south.

12 Platoon was now in the lead. Lieutenant John Page, who had taken over from the tragically killed Jim Barry, looked for the fence, running at right-angles to the ridge, that would guide him to the correct start-line for the assault. Unfortunately there was little left of the fence marked on the maps, and Corporal Barton's section, at the point of the platoon, could only find a few strands of wire to follow. The number of ice-covered ponds added to the difficulty and the intense cold was beginning to affect men's reactions, as they worked their way south to the western end of Wireless Ridge.

Once more, massive fire-power began to soften up the enemy, who apparently still had no intimation that they were about to be rolled up from a flank. The initial idea had been for D Company simply to sweep eastwards along the ridge without stopping, with 11 Platoon on the left, 12 Platoon on the right and 10 Platoon in reserve. There was still uncertainty as to whether Tumbledown to the south had been taken or not, and clearly a battle was still in progress on that mountain as the Scots Guards fought to drive out the Argentines on its summit. But Neame and his D Company had no intention other than to push on regardless, although they knew that if Tumbledown was still in enemy hands by daylight then 2 Para would be extremely vulnerable.

The bombardment of the western end of the Wireless Ridge continued as the platoons advanced. It seemed to have been effective, since no enemy were encountered at all, although, to be certain, 11 Platoon cleared any bunkers they came across on the reverse slope with grenades.

The first part of Wireless Ridge was now clear and across the dip, where the track came up, lay the narrower rocky outcrops of

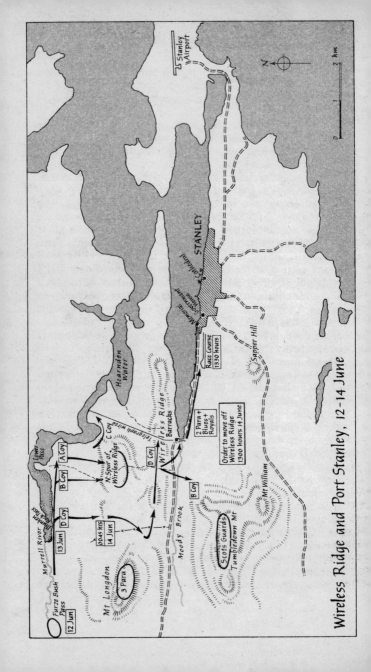

Wireless Ridge and Port Stanley, 12-14 June

The Argentine gun-line at Goose Green. The empty shell cases
show the amount of artillery fire 2 Para endured

Bluff Cove – the sole surviving Chinook,
three others had been lost on *Atlantic Conveyor*

Men of C Company at Bluff Cove

By Ron Binney's house at Fitzroy. Defensive positions behind
have been shored up with parts of his fences

Men of 2 Para boarding the LCU for the journey from
Bluff Cove to Fitzroy. After a cold, wet, three-hour journey
they found themselves back at Bluff Cove
A Company in the wool-shed at Fitzroy

Bluff Cove and its little settlement

8 June – men of 2 Para patrolling at Fitzroy,
with *Sir Galahad* burning fiercely in the background

Daybreak, 12 June, during the battalion's march from Mount Kent

Arriving at Furze Bush Pass

Looking south from Wireless Ridge to Moody Brook barracks

opposite above: Wireless Ridge

opposite below: The main ridge of Wireless Ridge with Port Stanley in the background on the right. D Company attacked in this direction

Recovery of 2 Para's dead by Scout helicopter on Wireless Ridge

The approach to Stanley

Captured Argentine 155-mm gun

Argentine prisoners on Stanley airfield after the surrender

Christ Church Cathedral, Port Stanley where on 15 June 2 Para
held a Service of Thanksgiving. The structure in front
of the Cathedral is made from the jaw-bones of whales

left to right: David Norris, *Daily Mail*; Brigadier Julian Thompson, RM, OC 3 Commando Brigade; Colour-Sergeant Cotton, 2 Para; Major Tony Rice, RA, the Battery Commander; Lieutenant-Colonel Hew Pike, OC 3 Para

Padre David Cooper (left) assisting with casualty evacuation

Captain Chris Dent, 2/IC A Company, talking to Robert Fox
of the BBC on Sussex Mountain

Captain Allan Coulson, 2 Para's Intelligence Officer,
with a captured Pucara at Goose Green

The RSM at Goose Green
on a cross-country
motorcycle borrowed
from one of
the inhabitants

Major Philip Neame,
OC D Company,
on board *Norland*

Major John Crosland, OC B Company, on Sussex Mountain
Captain Steve Hughes, the RMO, removing a soldier's tooth
on Sussex Mountain

left to right: Captain Mark Worsley-Tonks, who took over as Adjutant; Lieutenant-Colonel David Chaundler; Major Chris Keeble; RSM Simpson. They are standing in front of a captured Argentine gun, brought back to Britain

Captain David Wood, the Adjutant, on board *Norland*.
He was killed in action with A Company on Darwin Hill

below left: Captain Chris Dent, killed in action on Darwin Hill

below right: Jim Barry, OC 12 Platoon of D Company, killed under a white
flag in an incident during the battle for Goose Green

Lieutenant-Colonel Herbert ('H') Jones, OBE, OC 2 Para, killed in
action with A Company on Darwin Hill. Colonel Jones was
posthumously awarded the Victoria Cross for his
outstanding gallantry and leadership (*Cassidy and Leigh*)

Major-General John Frost (left) and Lieutenant-Colonel 'H' Jones
(*Cassidy and Leigh*)

the remainder of the objective. Fire was concentrated on these areas from A and B Companies as tanks, Milans and machine-guns provided an intense concentration on to three enemy machine-gun posts that remained.

Efforts to switch artillery support further forward and on to the area of Moody Brook had unfortunate results. Five rounds of high explosive crashed on to the ridge around and very near the leading D Company platoons. 3 Section of 11 Platoon was caught in the open and, despite screams to stop the firing, it was too late. Private Parr was killed instantly, and Corporal McAuley was somersaulted into some rocks, completely dazed, and had to be picked up by a stretcher party.

There was a considerable delay while a livid Major Neame tried to get the gunners to sort themselves out. It seemed that one gun was off target, as C Company had noted, but at the gun-lines they did not know which, since in the dark it was impossible to note the fall of shot, even if there had been time, and the other battery was not available owing to shortage of ammunition. In the meantime the CO was growing increasingly impatient, urging the D Company commander to press on.

As soon as the gunners could guarantee reasonable support, and with increased efforts from the Blues and Royals, Neame was off again. All through the wait constant harassing fire from the enemy had been landing around the company, so none were sorry to move. Despite the fire pouring on to the ridge-line ahead, enemy machine-gunners continued firing from well sited bunkers, and were still staunchly in action as the platoons advanced.

They moved with 11 Platoon on the left, 12 Platoon ahead on the ridge itself, with the company commander immediately behind and, in the rear, 10 Platoon. 12 Platoon came across an abandoned Argentine recoilless rifle, an anti-tank weapon, as they crossed the start-line, which may well have been the weapon that had earlier been engaging the tanks on the A and B Company positions. The platoon moved down into the gap between the two parts of the ridge line, but as the soldiers passed by some ponds, very heavy machine-gun fire began from their front and illumination was called for as the platoon answered the firing. Corporal Barton came across some orange string, possibly indicating a minefield, but his platoon commander urged him on regardless.

The enemy appeared to be surprised by the direction of the

assault, and as the Paras advanced, they could hear an Argentine voice calling out, possibly to give warning of this sudden attack from the west. 10 Platoon came across a lone enemy machine-gunner who lay wounded in both legs, his weapon lying abandoned beside him.

Corporal Harley of 11 Platoon caught his foot in a wire, which may have been part of a minefield, and, fearing that it might be an Argentine jumping mine, unravelled himself with some care. The platoon pushed on, skirmishing by sections until they met a concertina of wire. Fearing mines, Sappers were called for from Company Headquarters, but these could do little in the darkness except tape off the suspect area. In fact channels could be discerned between the concertinas, and these were assumed, correctly, as it turned out, to be safe lanes.

While 11 Platoon was extricating itself from the minefield, Neame pushed 12 Platoon on and brought 10 Platoon out to the left to maintain the momentum. Suddenly an intense burst of firing brought the company to a halt. It was a critical moment. For a short time, *all* commanders had to do everything in their power to get things going again, with platoon commanders and sergeants and section commanders all urging their men on. It was a real test of leadership as several soldiers understandably went to ground.

A brief fire-fight ensued, with 12 Platoon engaging the enemy as they pushed forward on the right overlooking Moody Brook below, where lights could be seen. The moment of doubt had passed, however, and once more the men were clearing bunkers and mopping up with gusto. 10 and 12 Platoons now moved on either side of the company commander. Maximum speed was needed to keep the enemy off balance as they fell back, conducting a fighting withdrawal along the ridge. The tanks continued to fire, directed by the company commander. Unfortunately his signaller had fallen into a shell hole and become separated, thus creating considerable frustration for the CO, who wanted to talk to Neame about the progress of his battle.

During 12 Platoon's brief fight Private Slough had been hit and died later in hospital, and another soldier was wounded.

Enemy artillery fire continued to make life uncomfortable. Fortunately D Company's task was no longer difficult, as most of the enemy bunkers had now been abandoned. 12 Platoon reached the telegraph wires and consolidated there, while the other platoons reorganised further back along the ridge. Shell fire intensified and snipers began to engage from enemy positions further to the east along the ridge.

Neame went up to see the platoon commander, Lieutenant Page. Snipers in the rocks were still firing on the platoon and it seemed that the enemy might be about to counter-attack from the direction of Moody Brook, to the right.

On several occasions the company commander was nearly hit, and his perambulations began to be the cause of some comment. Sergeant Meredith shouted to him, 'For God's sake push off, Sir—you're attracting bullets everywhere you go!'

100 metres or so to the east, Argentines could be heard shouting to each other, as though rallying for a counter-attack. John Page called for fire support, and then ordered his own men to stop firing, for by so doing they were merely identifying their positions. They felt very isolated and vulnerable.

For two very long and uncomfortable hours the company remained under pressure. Small-arms fire mingled with all types of HE fell in and around 12 Platoon's position as the men crouched in the abandoned enemy sangars and in shell holes. John Page continued to move around his platoon, organising its defences, and suffering a near-miss in the process. He was hit by a bullet, which passed between two grenades hanging on his webbing and landed in a full magazine in his pouch. He was blown off his feet by the shock. 'It was like being hit by a sledge-hammer and having an electric shock at the same time,' he later described the moment. As he lay there a round exploded in the magazine, but fortunately the grenades remained intact, and he was soon on his feet.

Meanwhile the CO was still trying to get in touch with Neame to know the form. Lieutenant Webster, OC 10 Platoon, was momentarily elevated to commanding the company since he was the only officer left near Company Headquarters. As he talked to the CO, voices could be heard below in the direction of Moody Brook. Corporal Elliot's section opened up and automatic fire was returned by perhaps ten to fifteen men. 11 Platoon moved forward to join 10 Platoon in a long extended line along the ridge, the men firing downhill towards the enemy position. Eventually the CO got through to the company commander, who had had a hair-raising time walking along the ridge to discover what was happening. He now informed the CO of his fears of imminent attack.

Sporadic enemy fire from Tumbledown added to D Company's danger, and all the earlier fears of the consequences of delay to the 5 Brigade attack came to the fore. The CO offered to send tanks up but Neame declined, since they would be very exposed on the forward slope fire positions they would be forced to adopt. He would have preferred another company to hold the first part of Wireless Ridge, which as yet remained undefended.

The company reorganised, leaving Corporal Owen's section forward as a standing patrol while 10 and 11 Platoons found dug-outs on the reverse slope. 12 Platoon stayed in its positions near the telegraph poles.

There was little more that the Companies on the northern spur could now do to support D Company. Two of A Company's trained medical orderlies had been wounded by the shelling that still continued, so the platoons had to look after their own casualties—once again the value of the medical training for all ranks was vindicated. Fortunately the helicopters in support that night were fully effective, evacuating casualties with minimum delay, and other casualties were taken back to the RAP on one of the tanks. The enemy artillery fire gave the remainder every incentive to dig, and the possibility of being overlooked by Mount Tumbledown in the morning was an additional spur.

For A and B Companies it was now a matter of lasting the cold night out, which was not without incident. Privates (Jud' Brookes and Gormley of A Company's 1 Platoon had been hit by shrapnel. The rule was to switch on the injured man's easco light, normally used for night parachute descents, to ensure that he would not be missed in the dark. Sergeant Barrett went back to look for Brookes, whose light was smashed.

'All right, Brookes—me and the Boss will be back to pick you up later.'

'Ee, Sarge,' he replied in a thick Northern accent, 'Ah knows tha f—— will.'

Unknown to them, the men of 3 Platoon were actually sitting next door to thirteen Argentine soldiers, who were taking cover from their own shell-fire. Only later in the morning were they found and taken prisoner.

In B Company, the state of Privates Carroll and Philpott of 5 Platoon was a cause for concern, since both were now suffering from hypothermia after being immersed in one of the ponds. Their section commander, Corporal Steve Curtis, decided to tell the platoon commander. As he ran out into the shelling, a round exploded close by, shredding his clothes almost completely yet, amazingly, leaving him unharmed.

The mortar teams had been busy all night. By now they had moved on to the side of the A and B Company hill to avoid shelling, which had been uncomfortably close at their first position in the bottom of the valley to the north. Improvised bins had helped to reduce the tendency of the mortar tubes to bed into the soft peat, although not completely, and another problem was that tubes would at times actually slip out of their base-plates under recoil. To prevent this, mortarmen took turns to stand on the base-plates as the tubes were fired, and by the end of the night four men had suffered broken ankles for their efforts. The fire they had been able to provide was very effective, however, and all concerned had been determined that, this time, there would be no question of running short of ammunition or of being out of range. The 3 Para mortars on Longdon did sterling work providing illumination.

The Machine-Gun Platoons, too, had been hard at work, their six guns providing intense heavy fire throughout the night. Re-supplied by the tanks and by the splendid work of WO2 Grace's Pioneer Platoon, they had had no worries about ammunition. But gradually the guns broke down, and by dawn only two of the six were still in action.

In Battalion Headquarters the second-in-command, the Operations Officer and Captain David Constance had taken turns at duty officer. At one point the second-in-command, Major Keeble, had been able to see the flashes of the enemy 155-mm guns as they fired, but no amount of reporting back produced any counter-measures. Once the drone of a low-flying Argentine Canberra jet was heard, and amidst the din of artillery even larger thuds reverberated as the aircraft dropped its bombs. Private Steele of the Defence Platoon was unlucky: as he lay on the ground a piece of shrapnel caught him in the back. He hardly felt it, thinking that it was only a piece of turf from the explosion—only later did he discover a rather nasty wound where the metal had penetrated.

The CO's party had not escaped either. A stray round hit Private McLoughlin, a member of the Battery Commander's group, and actually penetrated his helmet at the front. The helmet deflected the round, however, and McLoughlin walked away unharmed.

The snipers were in great demand. Their night-sights enabled them to identify the enemy infra-red sights and to use the signature that then appeared in the image itensifier as an aiming-mark. The Commando Sappers had had a relatively minor role to play in the battle, since there were no mines that it was imperative to clear. But, as at Goose Green, they provided a very useful addition when acting as infantry.

On Wireless Ridge at first light, 12 Platoon was still being sniped at from behind and to the right. Further back along the ridge, Corporal Owen had searched a command post. While rummaging in the bunker, he found a map showing all the details of the Argentine positions, as well as some patrol reports. These were quickly dispatched to Company Headquarters and on to Brigade.

Private Ferguson, in Owen's section, suddenly noticed four or five men below them. The corporal was uncertain as to who they could be—possibly 12 Platoon—and told Ferguson to challenge. The latter yelled 'Who's there!', and was instantly greeted with a burst of fire that left them in no doubt. Grenades started to explode around Owen and his men as the enemy counter-attacked. The section opened fire, and Corporal Owen shouted for the machine-guns to engage.

10 Platoon meanwhile were firing on either side of the section, and Owen himself blasted away with eight M-79 rounds. The section was soon short of ammunition, and the men began to ferret for abandoned Argentine supplies. Just then the remainder of the platoon moved up to join the section; though uncertain as to exactly where the enemy were, they were determined to prevent the Argentines from regaining the ridge.

Private Lambert heard an Argentine, close in, shouting, 'Grenado, grenado!'

'What a good idea,' he thought, and lobbed one of his own in the direction of the voice. There were no more shouts.

11 Platoon also saw a group of four men to its front. 2nd Lieutenant Chris Waddington was unable to make out who they

were and, thinking they might be 10 Platoon, shouted to them to stop. The four men took no notice, so he ordered a flare to be put up—the figures ran off as the platoon engaged with small arms and grenades. The orders not to exploit beyond the ridge-line meant that not all the enemy positions had been cleared during the night, and it seemed that some stay-behind snipers had been left there, and it was probably these that had given 12 Platoon so much trouble. But the counter-attack, such as it was, had fizzled out. Artillery fire was called down on Moody Brook to break up any further efforts at dislodging D Company. Down below the ridge a Landrover could be seen trying to get away. Lance-Corporal Walker fired at it and it crashed.

11 Platoon now came under extremely accurate enemy artillery fire, possibly registered on the flashes of their weapons. Major Neame therefore ordered them to cease firing with small arms, intending to continue the battle with artillery alone. Moody Brook was deserted, however. In the distance the men of D Company noticed two Argentine soldiers walking off down the track as if at the end of an exercise.

In the light of dawn it appeared to the Paras on the ridge that a large number of enemy troops were moving up to reinforce Sapper Hill to the south-east. Neame called for artillery with great urgency, but no guns were available. After a further twenty minutes or so, by which time the enemy had reached the top, the target was engaged. Meanwhile other Argentines could be seen streaming off Tumbledown and Harriet—5 Brigade had won its battles.

As D Company began to engage this new target the CO arrived. He confirmed Neame's orders to fire on the enemy retiring towards Stanley, and the company now joined in with machine-guns in a 'turkey shoot'. John Greenhalgh's helicopters swept in and fired SS-11 rockets and, together with two other Scouts, attacked an Argentine battery. The enemy AA was still active, however, and all the helicopters withdrew.

The retiring Argentines on Tumbledown had made no reply to the helicopters, and their artillery had stopped. It was obvious that a major change had occurred. The news was relayed to the Brigadier, who found it difficult to believe what was happening. But the CO realised how vital it was to get the battalion moving into Stanley before the enemy could rally, and A and B

Companies, together with the Blues and Royals, were ordered to move as fast as possible up on to Wireless Ridge. The Brigadier arrived, still disbelieving until Colonel Chaundler said, 'It's OK, Brigadier, it's all over.' Together they conferred as to what to do next. D Company ceased firing on the fleeing enemy on the far hillside, and the order was given that men were only to fire if fired upon first. Permission was then given for the battalion to move on.

B Company, by now on the ridge, was ordered down into Moody Brook. Corporal Connors's section of 5 Platoon led the way, still expecting to come under fire from the 'Triple As' on the race-course. The other two sections covered him forward. He cleared the flattened buildings of the old barracks and Curtis's section took over, clearing the bridge over the Murrell River and the building on the other side, while all the time their platoon commander was exhorted, 'Push on, push on!' They remained cautious, fearing booby traps or a sudden burst of fire.

A Company now took the lead as B Company, covering A's advance, moved south on to the high ground on the far side of the valley, above the road, passing through three abandoned gun positions on the way. The tanks of the Blues and Royals moved east along Wireless Ridge to give support if it should be necessary. A Company was well on the way down the road into Stanley, with C and D Companies following, when Brigade announced a cease-fire. Cheers went up, and red berets quickly replaced steel helmets. Bottles of alcohol miraculously appeared to celebrate with. Relief, elation, disbelief—all in turn had their effect.

Major Dair Farrar-Hockley led his men towards the race-course, past the abandoned guns that had been spotted so many hours earlier yet had remained operational in spite of requests for artillery fire. According to civilians afterwards, the Argentines still on the outskirts of Stanley simply broke and ran when they heard that 'the Paras' were coming. The leading elements of the battalion arrived in Stanley at 1330 hours, on Monday, 14 June some five hours before the official cease-fire, with 2nd Lieutenant Mark Coe's 2 Platoon the first into the town. They were the first British troops into the capital.

Eventually all the companies were brought into the western outskirts, finding shelter amongst the deserted houses, a few of which had suffered from stray shells. One or two dead Argentine soldiers still lay in the street where they had been caught by shell-fire. On the race-course the Argentine flag was pulled down and Sergeant-Major Fenwick's Union Jack once more served its purpose.

As the CO had said, it *was* all over, or almost. Advancing a little way into the town, D Company's Lieutenant Shaun Webster and Corporal Owen had reached the War Memorial. They decided to take a look at Government House, a little way ahead to the right of the road, and approached the building. There were staff cars and soldiers around the large house, and it appeared to be wired up for demolition, but an Argentine sergeant invited them in. A major appeared, saluting them both and shaking their hands, enquiring whether they were part of 'the advance party· In a sense, of course, they were.

The officer then said, 'Gentlemen, may I present General Menendez.' The Commander-in-Chief of the Argentine forces in the Falklands came through a door and saluted both Webster and Corporal Owen, and he too shook their hands. There were about ten other Argentine officers in the room with the General.

'What is happening?' Menendez asked. Lieutenant Webster did his best to explain the situation as far as he knew it, guessing mainly at what to say.

The General then asked how old they were—he had, he said, a twenty-five-year-old son somewhere on West Falkland—and next asked Webster which battalion he was from.

'You are from the 2nd Parachute Regiment? Ah yes, you fought our 1st Parachute Regiment on Wireless Ridge.' The General had confirmed what was already suspected from the documents captured on Wireless Ridge. 'We will be formally surrendering at 4 o'clock today.'

Finally, General Menendez thanked both men for their help, shook their hands again, and they parted.

An officer showed them to the door—the large front door. As the two soldiers emerged all the drivers of the staff cars came respectfully to attention. Ever mindful of security, Lieutenant Webster and Corporal Owen wondered, as they walked down the drive, whether they ought to be going backwards.

CHAPTER 8

The End Of It All

So 2 Para came to Port Stanley, exactly seven weeks after they had set sail upon *Norland*. The battle for the Falkland Islands was won. The battalion's casualties in the fighting for Wireless Ridge were three killed and eleven wounded, and it was thought that, of the enemy, 100 were killed, seventeen were taken prisoner and hundreds fled.

Stanley itself was not badly damaged, although it was marked by evidence of the occupation, and the battalion was sad to learn of the deaths of three local women through our own shelling, the only civilian deaths in the entire campaign. The town had been deliberately attacked by the British only once, in a daring, almost surgical strike by armed helicopters against Menendez's headquarters in the town hall.

To prevent an inadvertent clash between British and Argentine soldiers, British troops were to stay west of the War Memorial on the Harbour Road until all Argentines—of whom there were literally thousands—had withdrawn from Port Stanley itself. Surprisingly, no efforts were made that first night to ensure that the Argentines kept to their side of the bargain and they remained in the town, much to the consternation of the civilian population, with the inevitable breakdown of discipline. A certain amount of looting and arson took place.

So, on the following morning, several of the companies found themselves in a more familiar role, learned in Northern Ireland, conducting Internal Security tasks such as VCPs and town patrols. Fortunately no incidents occurred and the Argentines were gradually consolidated east of Stanley on the airfield to await repatriation.

On the afternoon of 15 June 2 Para marched through the streets of Port Stanley to a Service of Thanksgiving in the beautiful old stone cathedral in the centre of the town. The whole battalion was crammed into the relatively confined area, normally used by much smaller congregations; even the choir stalls were impressed to the full to seat the officers.

It was a moving and euphoric occasion, witnessed by the cameras of BBC Television. Padre David Cooper began his address amidst cheers and laughter. It was all over now, he said, we are safe again. 'But what,' he enquired 'did you really think about when you thought you were going to *die*? Was it your wife . . . your girlfriend . . . or even your dog? Or it may have been your own life itself.'

No one there could claim not to have been deeply affected by their experiences, and few could ignore David Cooper's efforts to put over the essence of his calling to a rather tough collection of soldiers such as those of 2 Para. Perhaps it was the way that the Padre was able to communicate, rather than what he said, that counted, and now his words were as fitting a summing-up as there could be.

Soon afterwards the battalion was busy again, searching Argentine prisoners as they queued endlessly for the ships now waiting to take them back to their country. Gradually each battalion was given time to recoup aboard the LSL *Sir Launcelot*, which had moored alongside the jetty. For most, this was the first hot shower or bath since leaving the *Norland*, while fresh bacon and eggs and not a few pints of beer did wonders for morale.

Sadly, even now discipline was not always as good as it should have been amongst the troops of the Task Force in Stanley. Looting of Argentine stocks, not to mention hijacking of our own supplies, grew to epidemic proportions, and the RSM mounted guards over the large containers that held the Argentine rations. In the end, General Moore was obliged to threaten severe penalties to anyone found guilty of such behaviour.

Battalion Headquarters had now been relocated in the local schoolhouse, where Argentine attempts to visit South American culture upon the children of the Falklands were much in evidence. Tapes of English music had been sealed, with labels affixed forbidding their playing on the school tape-recorder, and Argentine music had been substituted instead. Now, however, the haunting tones of the 'Pipes of Pan' played by Gheorghis Zamfir were soon echoing in the corridors, with the theme from *The Light of Experience* providing a fitting commentary upon the days that had passed.

By now *Norland* was in Stanley Harbour, and it was decided that 2 and 3 Para would travel back to Ascension Island together, with the heavy equipment following on the car ferry *Europic*, which had been requisitioned for the Task Force. There was to be one final act of remembrance.

On the last day, Friday, 25 June, as the ships were being loaded, two Chinook-loads of representatives from each company flew back over Bluff Cove and Fitzroy and on to land at the bottom of Darwin Hill, near the settlement that had been liberated seemingly so long ago. The inhabitants of Darwin and Goose Green had erected a black steel cross on a stone monument on top of the hill, just beyond the gorse-line, in memory of the men of the battalion group who had died to secure their freedom. The monument had been sited so that it was visible from both Goose Green and Darwin, starkly silhouetted on the hillside overlooking the remains of the Schoolhouse and other parts of the battlefield.

In the late afternoon of a cold winter's day, settlers and soldiers joined in a semi-circle as David Cooper once more conducted a short service in memory of the fallen. Down below, the gorse still smoked from the battle fought twenty-eight days before. Wreaths were laid. All stood in silence: Brigadier Julian Thompson, Lieutenant-Colonel David Chaundler, Lieutenant-Colonel Hew Pike of 3 Para, Commander Chris Esplin-Jones, who commanded the *Norland* Naval Party, Captain Don Ellerby, the Master of MV *Norland*, and his First Engineer, Bob Lough, Major Chris Keeble and the company commanders, and others.

Conclusion

There could be no doubt about the warmth of feeling within the nation for the Task Force. The farewells accorded to the troops leaving for the Falklands were without parallel in recent years, the papers, radio and television were throughout the campaign packed with items that had any bearing on the subject, and it became almost the sole topic of conversation when people came together. It ill behove anyone to speak out against the project, and doubters were wise to keep a low profile. We all believed that our men were going to a part of the world where the climate alone was lethal, and that the privations they would suffer would be almost unendurable. No such manifestations of sympathy had been accorded to the British soldiers who had been sent to Korea not many years before, where the conditions under which men had to live in the winter really were severe. Moreover, they had faced a foe who was utterly ruthless and many times more formidable than the Argentines, and the fate of anyone who fell into their hands could be quite horrific.

Perhaps much of the 'Falklands' enthusiasm was due to the media. In 1936, when trouble arose in Palestine, now the state of Israel, the whole of the 1st Division was sent there at very short notice. The Category A reservists were called up to fill the ranks, and several liners were requisitioned to take the troops. It was all done within a week and was a splendid example of improvisation, yet there was practically no public interest, and certainly no acclamation of any kind. The outcome was that when the Arab rebellion had been quelled, the soldiers returned almost unnoticed.

Now the media, particularly television, brings the reality of the way our servicemen live into every home. The services must recognise this public face, and give to it their earnest attention in the future. Soldiers may no longer be alone on distant hillsides, for their every action may be seen by those around the fireside at home, and every decision made by the commanders queried and discussed by the experts in clubs and pubs. We have to realise that although some of the criticism that arises will be carping, much more goodwill and support for the services will be generated than would be the case if there were no reporting. People want to know, but those responsible will have the most delicate task in deciding what can be told and what not. Certainly during the Falklands campaign there were at times what amounted to most serious breaches of security, and the lives of servicemen were jeopardised thereby. But, on the other hand, the understanding, the kindness and the generosity of the people of Britain to their servicemen was an example to the rest of the world.

For the servicemen, the Falklands campaign threw up problems that did not necessarily reach the ears of those at home. All the soldiers spoken to were unanimous in condemning the army boot as being quite unsuitable for the campaign, and it has been said that this inadequacy was responsible for more casualties than enemy action. Undoubtedly the Argentine soldiers were better shod than our men. An article in a recent issue of the *British Army Journal* describes how British soldiers arrived to fight the battle of Omdurman in 1898 with bare feet, their boots having disintegrated on the way—plainly this is no new problem. No sportsman, farmer, or any countryman, reckons that he can pursue all his activities with one type of footwear (although the gumboot goes a long way to being the universal item), but the appropriate footgear is essential to all who would do things properly. There are problems, of course, because feet are of different shape and sizes, but it is pointless to spend several thousand pounds in arming a man if he becomes ineffective through failure to spend twenty or thirty pounds in covering his feet.

It was strange that use was not made earlier of the support available from the weapons of the two troops of the Blues and the Royals, for their effect during the battle of Wireless Ridge was considerable. Major Keeble had tried to get them for the Goose Green venture but had been told that they were not available, although they were not used for anything else, then or for several days. It seems that they were added to the Task Force as an afterthought, and that no one further up the chain of command appears to have appreciated their cross-country capability, or the skill and tenacity of their crews. Perhaps the information, largely wrong, shown on the 'going' map prevented the brigade commander from deciding to use them until they had been proved in such terrain.

The last thing one would wish to do would be to decry the gallantry and skill of the SAS, but there were times when their presence, or alleged presence, in 2 Para's battle area limited the battalion's ability to patrol where and how it wished. Furthermore, some of the information given to the battalion was optimistic to a degree, and one wonders whether the priorities of the roles now given to that splendid body of men are correct. Offensive action by the SAS seems to have become more important than target acquisition, but it is the latter task which, if carried out successfully, can pay far higher dividends. In carrying out this task, the small sub-units concerned, with their excellent communications, should be able to glean and deliver priceless information which cannot be produced from any other source.

It was not surprising that air support was inadequate, since obviously most of what was available had to protect the ships that had brought the Task Force. But the allocation of helicopter support seems to have been disappointing, however, for when 2 Para was the only unit in action, when one would have thought that they would be given priority, this had not by any means been the case. One of the major tragedies was the loss of *Atlantic Conveyor*, the ship carrying the Chinook helicopters. Only one survived, and its usefulness was immeasurable. One wonders whether it was wise to put so many valuable aircraft on one vessel, for had they been available, the options open to the command would have allowed for far better time-saving plans. Indeed, some offensive airborne operations might have obviated the need to attack some of the quite formidable defensive features that, in the end, had to be dealt with conventionally, often with heavy casualties.

As in every campaign that ever was and ever will be fought, there were shortcomings and mistakes at brigade level, but considering how the two headquarters were sent off at such short notice, and how the Commando Brigade had to cope with the addition of two major units while 5 Brigade was cobbled together with units it had never seen before, it is remarkable that both headquarters performed so well. They did in fact succeed in what they had set out to do, and it ill behoves anyone to be too critical of the officers who bore the responsibility. The arrangements were far from being ideal, however, and had the opposition been firmer we might well have had to tell a different story today. Only a few short years ago there existed a formation called the 3rd Division, which was tailor-made for exactly the sort of emergency as the Falklands. There was also a complete parachute brigade group ready and available, and another infantry brigade.

These timely arrangements were abolished when the government of the day demanded economy, and those responsible for implementing it decided that it was better to disband headquarters than any of the fighting units. Brigade headquarters were abolished throughout the Army, and divisional headquarters were ordered to take over direct command of no less than ten and up to fifteen major units. It was a system that did not work from the start, and senior officers employed every kind of artifice in trying to keep an intermediate command set-up. After tremendous disruption and, indeed, more useless expense, the brigade headquarters have been reinstated. One must hope that such dangerous and harmful expedients are never allowed in the future, and one must be thankful that no really grave emergency arose while our army was struggling to cope with a system of command in disarray. It may be that the trouble is that after a few years without a major war the uninitiated obtain positions of power and responsibility, where they are able to think up, recommend and then institute dangerous and ineffective measures which will satisfy politicians who are determined on economy by any means, and who will not look too deeply into the end result.

It could be claimed, however, that at the time the nation's overall policy was to concentrate on our defensive alliance with NATO, in the belief that we would never again embark on expeditions outside Europe on our own. In which case, and if such a policy could be rigidly adhered to in all circumstances, then it could also be claimed that there never would be a need for 'fire brigades'. But Falklands episodes have a way of arriving to upset the most determined intentions, and the nation will want to feel that wherever our soldiers may be sent, their subsequent employment will be in the best possible hands, and that those hands have the best possible means of conducting their affairs.

In the very dangerous world in which we live, we need, perhaps, an urgent reappraisal of our defence policies, so that all the possible danger spots outside NATO can be re-examined. Where there are people of our own kith and kin, or anyone who can claim our protection, in dangerous outposts, they should be brought back into the fold where they can be protected at less expense to the British taxpayer. Those preferring to risk their futures should, of course, be allowed to do so. But when it costs such prodigious sums to protect our own vital interests, and even then only by the barest possible margin, it does not make sense to spend millions near Cape Horn, especially since it is the oil route round the Cape of Good Hope that is vital. If the protection of 1,800 or so Falklanders is going to require the construction of an airfield costing £300,000,000, it would seem to be far better to re-accommodate the islanders in similar circumstances nearer home, and spend the money on an airfield which could be used to deter our real enemies closer to Britain. And if the goodwill of all the people of South America is important, would it not be sensible to be magnanimous in victory, and to take a long hard look at the Argentine claims? Although few now disagree with the full justification of our cause in ejecting an unlawful invader from our land, wherever it may be, the circumstances bearing on this particular freehold are most certainly not sufficiently sanctified as to warrant further bloodshed. The men of 2 Para and of all the other Task Force units will always be ready to go where the government sends them, and to do again what they did before, but they should only be committed to where our true interests lie, and to where the danger to the realm lies.

The list of honours and awards made after the campaign brought joy and comfort to many, and disappointment to others. It was ever so. One was brought up in the tradition that it was vulgar to discuss awards for bravery at all, and the rather

haphazard system was regarded by old soldiers as the manifesta-
tion of an Act of God. But at the end of the Falklands campaign
the awards of two VCs were almost promulgated by the press.
These two particular actions had been so outstanding that
anyone with a means of communicating was almost bound to
draw attention to them, and it was a short step from that to
virtually writing the citations.

There always will be mistakes and omissions because we are all
but human. The reader, in following the fortunes of 2 Para, will
have noted the rather outstanding performances of some of the
actors, as it were, and may well have been surprised when
turning to the list of awards to note that they have received scant
or no official recognition. I believe that the Commander-in-Chief
has said that the co-ordination and final recommendations of the
awards for the campaign was the most difficult and arduous task
of the whole expedition.

None of this would matter if the winning of awards for
gallantry was merely the presentation, the subsequent wearing of
the gong and the ribbon, and the privilege of having rather
glamorous letters permanently behind one's name while one was
in the service. But now the making of such awards is something
that is for ever. Not only in life, but after it, for the children will
always take pleasure in being able to say that father was a 'so and
so'. Every nation has a different system and one would like to see
an objective study undertaken of the whole business. The most
impressive arrangements for awards were those of the regimental
battle honours after the two world wars. These were drawn up by
committees after extensive study of all the relevant factors, and
there were few who disagreed with their solutions. Although it
should always be possible for immediate awards to be made when
there can be no possible doubt about the merit of the action, it
might be that an independent committee would be able to delve
and confirm, or otherwise, more comprehensively than the
hard-pressed commanders in the field.

If the campaign in the Falkland Islands could be said to have had
at least one really beneficial result, it is in the confirmation of the
abilities of the modern generation of servicemen, and of the
Parachute Regiment in particular. Up till then, although the
Regiment's performances in Northern Ireland, Egypt, Cyprus

and several other theatres had been noteworthy, they had not had to face the hard pounding and rigours of real warfare conducted with modern weapons. From the foregoing chapters the reader will be able to draw his own conclusion, and decide where the Regiment stands.

APPENDIX I

Roll of Honour

Officers and men of the 2nd Battalion, The Parachute Regiment killed in action on the Falkland Islands.

Lieutenant-Colonel Herbert Jones, OBE	Commanding Officer
Captain C. Dent	Second-in-command, A Company
Captain D. A. Wood	Adjutant
Lieutenant J. A. Barry	D Company
Colour Sergeant G. P. M. Findlay	A Company
Corporal D. Hardman	A Company
Corporal S. R. Prior	A Company
Corporal P. S. Sullivan	D Company
Lance-Corporal G. D. Bingley	D Company
Lance-Corporal A. Cork	D Company
Lance-Corporal N. R. Smith	D Company
Private S. J. Dixon	D Company
Private M. W. Fletcher	D Company
Private M. H. Holman-Smith	HQ Company
Private S. Illingsworth	B Company
Private T. Mechan	D Company
Private D. A. Parr	D Company
Private P. Slough	D Company

Attached arms

Lieutenant R. J. Nunn, RM	Army Air Corps
Corporal D. Melia	Royal Engineers

APPENDIX II

Citation—The Victoria Cross

Lieutenant-Colonel Herbert Jones, OBE, The Parachute Regiment

On 28 May 1982 Lieutenant-Colonel Jones was commanding 2nd Battalion The Parachute Regiment on operations on the Falkland Islands. The Battalion was ordered to attack enemy positions in and around the settlements of Darwin and Goose Green. During the attack against an enemy, who was well dug in with mutually supporting positions sited in depth, the battalion was held up just south of Darwin by a particularly well prepared and resilient enemy position of at least 11 trenches on an important ridge. A number of casualties was received. In order to read the battle fully and to ensure that the momentum of his attack was not lost, Colonel Jones took forward his reconnaissance party to the foot of a re-entrant which a section of his battalion had just secured. Despite persistent, heavy and accurate fire the reconnaissance party gained the top of the re-entrant, at approximately the same height as the enemy positions. From here Colonel Jones encouraged the direction of his battalion mortar fire, in an effort to neutralise the enemy positions. However, these had been well prepared and continued to pour effective fire onto the battalion advance, which, by now held up for over an hour and under increasingly heavy artillery fire, was in danger of faltering.

In his effort to gain a good viewpoint, Colonel Jones was now at the very front of his battalion. It was clear to him that desperate measures were needed in order to overcome the enemy position and rekindle the attack, and that unless these measures were taken promptly the battalion would sustain increasing casualties and the attack perhaps even fail. It was time for personal leadership and action. Colonel Jones immediately seized a sub-machine gun, and, calling on those around him and with total disregard for his own safety, charged the nearest enemy position. This action exposed him to fire from a number of trenches.

As he charged up a short slope at the enemy position he was seen to fall and roll backward downhill. He immediately picked himself up, and again charged the enemy trench, firing his sub-machine gun and seemingly oblivious to the intense fire directed at him. He was hit by fire from another trench which he outflanked, and fell dying only a few feet from the enemy he had assaulted. A short time later a company of the battalion attacked the enemy, who quickly surrendered. The devastating display of courage by Colonel Jones had completely undermined their will to fight further.

Thereafter the momentum of the attack was rapidly regained, Darwin and Goose Green were liberated, and the battalion released the local inhabitants unharmed and forced the surrender of some 1,200 of the enemy.

The achievements of 2nd Battalion The Parachute Regiment at Darwin and Goose Green set the tone for the subsequent land victory on the Falklands. They achieved such a moral superiority over the enemy in this first battle that, despite the advantages of numbers and selection of battle-ground, they never thereafter doubted either the superior fighting qualities of the British troops, or their own inevitable defeat. This was an action of the utmost gallantry by a commanding officer whose dashing leadership and courage throughout the battle were an inspiration to all about him.

APPENDIX III

Honours and Awards

Officers and men of the 2nd Battalion, The Parachute Regiment who received honours and awards as a result of actions during the campaign to liberate the Falkland Islands, 21 May-14 June 1982.

Victoria Cross
Lieutenant-Colonel H. Jones, OBE (posthumous)
Distinguished Service Order
Major C. P. B. Keeble
Military Cross
Major J. H. Crosland
Major C. D. Farrar-Hockley
Lieutenant (now Captain) C. S. Connor
Distinguished Conduct Medal
Sergeant J. C. Meredith
Corporal D. Abols
Private S. Illingsworth (posthumous)
Military Medal
Sergeant T. I. Barrett
Corporal T. J. Camp
Corporal T. W. Harley
Lance-Corporal S. A. Bardsley
Lance-Corporal M. W. C. Bentley
Lance-Corporal G. D. Bingley (posthumous)
Lance-Corporal L. J. L. Standish
Private G. S. Carter
Private B. J. Grayling

Mention in Despatches
Major P. Neame
Captain (now Major) the Rev D. Cooper, Royal Army Chaplain's
 Department
Captain P. R. Farrar
Acting-Captain (now Captain) M. S. H. Worsley-Tonks
Captain S. J. Hughes, Royal Army Medical Corps
Lieutenant J. D. Page
Lieutenant G. R. Weighell
2nd Lieutenant G. Wallis
Sergeant I. Aird
Corporal D. Hardman (posthumous)
Lance-Corporal N. J. Dance
Lance-Corporal K. P. Dunbar
Private S. J. Alexander
Private A. E. Brooke
Private M. W. Fletcher (posthumous)
Private D. Gray
Private A. Mansfield
Private R. P. G. Morrell
Private E. O'Rourke

Awards to others involved with 2 Para during the Falklands
campaign.

Knight Commander of the Order of the Bath
Major-General J. J. Moore, RM, Commander, LFFI
Companion of the Order of the Bath
Brigadier J. H. Thompson, RM, OC 3 Commando Brigade
Commander of the Order of the British Empire
Captain D. A. Ellerby, Master, MV *Norland*
Officer of the Order of the British Empire
Captain W. J. C. Clarke, Master, MV *Europic*
Commander C. J. Esplin-Jones, RN, OC Naval Party, MV
Norland
Member of the Order of the British Empire
Major C. M. Davies, RE
J. R. R. Fox Esq, BBC
Distinguished Flying Cross
Captain J. G. Greenhalgh, RCT, attached Army Air Corps

Lieutenant R. J. Nunn, RM, attached Army Air Corps (posthumous)
Mention in Despatches
Major P. H. Gullan, MBE, MC, HQ 3 Commando Brigade
Lieutenant C. R. Livingstone, RE

The officers and men of 3 Para received twenty-four awards. This battalion made an arduous march clear across East Falkland in a remarkably swift time, and on the night of 11/12 June fought a long and bitter battle for Mount Longdon against well armed Argentine troops fighting from a complex of well prepared and sited defensive positions. By daylight the feature was in 3 Para's hands, but at a cost to the battalion of seventeen killed and forty wounded. The awards were: one Victoria Cross, one DSO, two MCs, two DCMs, three MMs, fourteen Mentions in Despatches, and one MBE.

For its part in the campaign, the Parachute Regiment has been awarded four battle honours: 'Falkland Islands 1982', 'Goose Green', 'Mount Longdon', and 'Wireless Ridge'. The first of these will be borne upon the Regimental Colours.

APPENDIX IV

Major Keeble's Ultimatum

Text of the message sent, in English and Spanish, to the Argentine commanders in Goose Green on the morning of 29 May 1983.

To The Commander Argentinian Armed Forces (Darwin) (Goose Green)
From Commander British Armed Forces (Darwin) (Goose Green Area)

Military Options:
We have sent a POW to you under a white flag of truce to convey the following military options:

1. That you unconditionally surrender your force to us by leaving the township, forming up in a military manner, removing your helmets and laying down your weapons. You will give prior notice of this intention by returning the POW under the white flag with him briefed as to formalities no later than 0830 hours local time.

2. You refuse in the first case to surrender and take the inevitable consequence. You will give prior notice of this intention by returning the POW without his flag (although his neutrality will be respected) no later than 0830 hours local.

3. In any event and in accordance with the terms of the Geneva Conventions and Laws of War you shall be held responsible

for the fate of any civilians in (Darwin) (Goose Green) and we
in accordance with these laws do give you prior notice of our
intention to bombard (Darwin) (Goose Green).

> Signed
> C KEEBLE
> Commander of the British Forces

Appendix V

The Brigade Log—Goose Green

Summary taken from the Log kept at HQ, 3 Commando Brigade from 27 May to 29 May 1982, during 2 Para's battles for Darwin and Goose Green.

27 0513 Air request to Brigade: A. Search for targets to destroy first priority gun line. B. Time on target 1200–2000. C. Not within 100 metres. D. Fortune? on ground 613B. E. Yes. F. As available. G. x 2. H. As available. J. Nil.

0826 From Brigade to 2 PARA. At present air is out due to weather. No Naval Gunfire Support as ship withdrawn before first light.

1400 Air request from 2 PARA. [Argentine] Company positions: GR 650614, 642600, 633586. Platoon positions: 663610: vehicle + guns 653595 troops in ? 651599.

1530 2 PARA C/S [Recce Platoon] contact GR 6563. C/S 32 fired on and forced to withdraw.

1540 Contact 656263 [should have been 653626!] C/S 32E fired on from south of Camilla Creek.

1621 First Harrier mission went in.

1631 New enemy position 660626; air strike at 1654. Visibility good.

1705 PARA RMO asked for medical resup. Can Brigade deliver?

1708 Air strike. Mission good.

	1727	C/S 32 and 32E broke contact. No casualties.
	2038	First sheldrake asset [ie guns] en route.
28	0652	A Company had engaged enemy at Burntside. Not a lot of fire returned. C/S ? closing up. B Company moving on to its objective.
	0702	From A Echelon [Camilla Creek House]. Problems of resupply. Request a snowcat from first light.
	0714	A Company on objective. B Company attacking.
	0714	From Brigade. Low cloud cover prevents movement of all helicopters until first light.
	0727	A Company on its objective. No casualties. No enemy. B Company 400 metres to go; no firing as yet.
	0741	B Company contact. 6–8 enemy dead.
	1742	B Company just short of PURPLE.
	0743	Brigade reports shortage of fuel for volvos. Was it for move of SAA? Yes.
	0800	B Company successfully taken objective. 5 enemy dead; remainder ran away.
	0821	A Company pushing on. All going well.
	0840	B Company going for D Company task towards GREEN.
	0912	Brigade liaison officer under artillery fire. Up to *200*? prisoners. (?)
	0914	D Company pushing forward. 2 enemy dead.
	0925	B Company holding. D Company pushing through from GREEN.
	0937	B(?) Company held up by machine-gun post, manoeuvring to left flank. Going well.
	0943	Two casualties in D Company. C Company moving forward and have established a position short of D Company. 8 prisoners and 2 dead.
	0945	Helicopter required at first light for casualties.
	0950	'Fun and games'. Close control. D Company sustained two casualties. Will need stretchers and helicopter.
	1014	Helicopter tasked from A Echelon to go direct to casualties at the RAP.
	1015	On GREEN, heading for BLACK. B Company passed through D Company on the right.

1030 Now going for BLACK.

1039 From CO 'On schedule and approaching PLACE FREE' [Darwin].

1101 Question from 2 PARA. Are enemy dead to be buried?

1127 A Company firm on BLACK(?) C Company leading element heading for WHITE(?).

1130 A-B Companies have now disengaged(?). C Company pushing down the middle towards WHITE 1000 metres south of BLACK.

1135 What time is the helicopter due for course? Reply from Brigade that aircraft are now en route.

1155 A Echelon now under air attack. One aircraft destroyed.

1156 Request for FGA support/top cover.

1159 Weather held on top cover.

1200 Three Pucaras attacked A Echelon. No damage, no kills.

1217 Brigade warns of more Pucaras approaching.

1236 Brigade asked if resupply was required. No it wasn't.

1259 All companies now between WHITE and BLACK. B Company engaging enemy 1000 metres south of BLACK.

1305 Pucaras now over our forward companies.

1309 Re-request for more artillery ammunition asked for yesterday. Air Raid Warning Red, but the ammunition is coming.

1328 B Company engaging enemy at 635592. C and D Companies pushing down ridge.

1331 CO injured, 2IC taking over.

1333 Request to Brigade for a helicopter to pick up the CO. All aircraft back at Brigade Headquarters for refuelling.

1340 Brigade have briefed new pilots to call at A Echelon, then to go forward to pick up the CO.

1347 Enemy position identified GR 634591 Boca House. Request air strike ASP.

1353 Brigade warned 2 PARA of change to Sea King helicopters during resupply to 2 PARA mortar. Badly shot up last time.

1358 Air Raid Warning Red on Darwin and Goose Green in two minutes' time passed by Brigade.

1400 From Brigade. No FGA available.

1402 Brigade trying to get two loads of mortar ammunition forward.

1421 HELARM request on Boca House. Attack from NNW. FLOT on BLACK. HELARM to be on standby.

1422 Request to Brigade: Where is the 'D' callsign [ie small helicopter for CO]?

1427 Grid 655617 now secure for course of CO.

1427 Brigade informs 2 PARA that enemy mortar are just about to be fixed on Darwin/Goose Green runway.

1435 Small helicopters en route to A Echelon, but slowly due to weather. They will regain briefing. [Had actually arrived by now to be briefed by RSO.]

1445 'D' callsign has begun task to pick up CO.

1451 Under air attack at A Echelon by Pucaras. Gazelle shot down; medics sent over to investigate [this was the helicopter going to pick up the CO in which Lieutenant Nunn was killed].

1511 Information from Brigade that Darwin/Goose Green airfield to be bombed soon. CO now reported dead.

1531 Request for 80% HE, 20% smoke for mortar.

1533 Weather conditions in area: low cloud on crests of hills.

1543 Enemy appear to be surrendering.

1609 About to engage Pucara on airfield with artillery.

1613 Enemy have surrendered on BLACK. Now moving to WHITE. Brigade informed 2 PARA that Pucara on airfield was probably damaged one.

1640 Brigade reassures 2 PARA that the mortar resupply will be done soon.

1643 A(?) Company on edge of airfield.

1647 Support Company had reported lots of white flags.

1650 Request for more Milans.

1656 All going well.

1659 Do 2 PARA still need the 'callsign in support' (HELARM)? No.

1728 One 'V' [Sea King] now at A Echelon. To be used for

casualties. No further helicopters available. Five medium and large ? loads to be carried by 'C' callsign.

1738   Milan ammunition to be moved in due course.

1751   100 POWs en route to A Echelon.

1756   Brigade Commander asks if reinforcements are required. No, but 2 PARA will let him know if they are.

1800   Brigade realises that BV 202s [Volvos] are at A Echelon [the snowcats hijacked from Sussex Mountain!]. Milan now available, but only two Milan can be moved at a time.

1809   Enemy target 649558, east of Goose Green Settlement. No FAC can be found. Brigade LO [Major Gullan] attempts to find FAC.

1840   B Company now west of Goose Green. C Company and D Company attacking from north-east. A Company in reserve.

1900   2 PARA ordered to clear enemy position, to hold, no withdrawal unless ordered by Brigade Headquarters. A company of 42 Commando is moving forward if required by 2 PARA.

1919   Commando company has departed for A Echelon.

1936   3 x Sea King left with company 42 Commando to A Echelon.

1949   B, C, D Companies around buildings and backed up by Support Company. Enemy are wavering. Require batteries, rations and ammunition. 150+ POWs, and some own casualties.

2003   Two Pucaras in area Goose Green.

2009   Pucara shot down. Pilot captured.

2012   1 x Huey, 1 x Chinook, 1 x Pucara approaching from north-west.

2017   Callsign 4 of 42 Commando have now left their location.

2159   From 2 PARA. 6 casualties outstanding: 4 x stretcher, 1 x stretcher Priority One and one sitting Priority One.

2240   Casualty evacuation task accepted by Brigade. Should be in soon.

	2244	From CO 2 PARA. Victor callsign [Sea King] must be on 60 minutes' call as not all casualties are in yet.
	2337	From 2 PARA. *No* helicopter has been forward. 4 casualties suffering from cold.
	2350	Report from 2 PARA. A helicopter came over and hovered for fifteen minutes.
	2359	Brigade report they have located the helicopter [a Sea King] but were unable to get it in again.
	0100	From 2 PARA: one of the wounded casualties will not survive unless evacuated; also two enemy require evacuation.
	0112	Brigade agree to one more run only.
29	1417	All over—coming out.
	1450	Air Force surrender.

APPENDIX VI

Message to 2 Para from the CGS

Text of a signal sent to 2 Para on 30 May 1982 by the Chief of the General Staff, General Sir Edwin Bramall, GCB, OBE, MC, ADC (Gen) (now Field-Marshal Sir Edwin Bramall, Chief of the Defence Staff).

TO RHQ PARA
DEPOT PARA
FOR COLONEL OF THE REGIMENT AND PARA-
CHUTE REGIMENT DEPOT FROM CHIEF OF THE
GENERAL STAFF PD GREATLY GRIEVE THE LOSS
OF COLONEL JONES CMM HIS ADJUTANT AND THE
OTHER 9 DEAD AND 26 WOUNDED* OF THE GAL-
LANT 2ND BATTALION CLN BUT WANTED YOU TO
KNOW HOW IMMENSELY HIGHLY I AND MY COL-
LEAGUES ON THE ARMY BOARD RATE THE PER-
FORMANCE OF THE BATTALION AGAINST AN
ENEMY OVER DOUBLE THEIR NUMBER CMM
DETERMINED TO STAND AND FIGHT PD NOT
ONLY WAS THE TASK GIVEN THE BATTALION OF
VITAL AND URGENT IMPORTANCE TO OUR COUN-
TRYS INTERESTS AND FUTURE AT THIS TIME BUT
ALSO IN ACHIEVING ALL ITS OBJECTIVES IN A TEN
HOUR BATTLE AFTER LOSING THE CO AND CAP-
TURING OVER 1200 PRISONERS THE BATTALION
HAS EXECUTED A FEAT OF ARMS AND GALLAN-

* Later confirmed as fifteen dead and thirty wounded.

TRY PROBABLY UNSURPASSED IN THE GLORIOUS HISTORY OF THE BRITISH ARMY PD IT WILL CERTAINLY RATE WITH THE OTHER GREAT EXAMPLES OF COURAGE BY THE PARACHUTE REGIMENT SUCH AS THE NORMANDY LANDINGS AND ARNHEM PD I SEND YOU ON BEHALF OF THE ARMY BOARD OUR WARMEST CONGRATULATIONS CMM WHICH IN DUE COURSE I HOPE CAN BE PASSED TO THE BATTALION CMM WHILST AT THE SAME TIME OFFERING YOU OUR DEEPEST SYMPATHY FOR THE LOSS OF SUCH FINE AND GALLANT OFFICERS AND MEN

In June General Bramall visited 2 and 3 Para aboard *Norland*, then in Ascension Island on the journey home. He made an address to the assembled soldiers, expressing the praise and gratitude of everyone for the two battalions' outstanding service in the Falklands—'In the years ahead, when you are old men . . . you will be able to say, as they said after Waterloo, after Alamein and Arnhem, "I marched, and fought, and won in the Falklands, and showed to the world the incomparable quality of professionalism of the British Army and the spirit and strength of the regimental system".'

Glossary

AA—Anti-aircraft

'A' Echelon—A battalion's forward supply unit dealing with replenishment of supplies, stores, ammunition, casualty evacuation etc

'Airborne snake'—A column of Airborne soldiers on the march

Air-burst—The effect of a shell fused to explode in the air, rather than on contact

AT—Anti-tank

'B' Echelon—A battalion's main re-supply unit, under the Quartermaster, dealing with supply forward to 'A' Echelon, and responsible for replenishment from depots etc

BC—Battery Commander (artillery)

Bergen—Pack carried by British infantry on active service, containing mess-kit, sleeping-bag etc

Blowpipe—Wire-guided ground-to-air missile fired from the shoulder. Operated by a team of two, Blowpipe is designed for use against aircraft attacking head-on or nearly so; it is less successful in flanking shots at fast jets, or at departing aircraft

'Boss'—Soldier's slang for platoon or company commander

CAP—Combat Air Patrol—anti-intrusion patrols maintained, in the Falklands, by Harriers

Chinook—Large twin-rotor helicopter with heavy lifting capability, used by both sides. For a considerable time the Task

Force operated only one Chinook, three others having gone down on *Atlantic Conveyor*.

CO—Commanding Officer

CSM—Company Sergeant-Major

CVR(T)—Combat Vehicle Reconnaissance (Tracked)—Scorpion and Scimitar tanks operated in the Falklands by two troops of the Blues and Royals (RHG/D)

Dead ground—Ground into which the enemy cannot fire because of land features between target and weapon

Direct fire, direct-fire weapons—Aimed fire brought to bear by a battalion in assault, eg with Milan, 66-mm rockets etc. As opposed to indirect (supporting) fire, eg artillery, mortars, naval gunfire, laid down to confuse, harass and distract the enemy

DMS—Director of Medical Services

DS—Directing Staff

Easco light—light carried by British parachute troops on their equipment, used during night jumps

84—84-mm anti-tank rocket, fired from a tube. Also known as Carl Gustav

FAC—Forward Air Controller. Officer (usually) on the ground who maintains a link by wireless between a land unit and aircraft attacking in support.

FN—Fabrique Nationale. Belgian arms company manufacturing the self-loading rifle, on which the British issue rifle is based.

FOO—Forward Observation Officer. Officer (usually) sent forward to observe for artillery units, relaying corrections to aim by wireless as the shell-fall is spotted

Forward slope—The slope of a hill facing the enemy, in other words exposed to enemy fire

G Ops—General Staff Operations

GPMG—General Purpose Machine-Gun. Rifle calibre (7.62-mm), belt-fed, the standard section armament of a parachute battalion's rifle companies, usually two per section. Designed by FN

Harrier—British jet-powered vertical take-off strike aircraft

HE—High Explosive (of shells, as opposed to armour-piercing, smoke etc)

Hexamine—Small solid fuel burner used to heat food, tea etc and carried by British infantrymen

HMS—Her Majesty's Ship

Huey—American-built helicopter used by Argentine forces

IO—Intelligence Officer

LCU—Landing Craft Unit. Large landing-craft, four of which were carried by each of the two assault ships (LPDs) in the Task Force, HMSs *Fearless* and *Intrepid*

LCVP—Landing Craft Vehicle and Personnel. Small landing-craft, four carried by each assault ship.

Lift—Helicopter airlift or, colloquially, a helicopter

LMG—Light machine-gun

LPD—Landing Platform Dock. Troop-carrying armed assault ship, equipped with landing-craft which can embark and disembark troops from a sea dock within the ship. LPDs are also equipped for helicopter lift, and are manned by officers and men of the Royal Fleet Auxiliary

LSL—Landing Ship Logistic. Lightly armed troop-carrying ships equipped for helicopter operation, RFA manned. *Sir Tristram* and *Sir Galahad* were LSLs

LUP—Lying-up place. Area for holding a body of troops, screened from the enemy, before an advance or assault

M-79—A grenade-launcher used by British troops

Main HQ—As opposed to Tac HQ, the battalion's headquarters dealing with administration during an action. Usually reasonable permanent until the battalion moves on, and very often based with 'A' Echelon

MFC—Mortar Fire Controller—soldier forward with a unit in action, equipped with radio to correct and adjust fire of support mortars

MFO—Military Forwarding Officer

Milan—Wire-guided anti-tank missile carried by infantry battalions, and very effective against fixed defences. Fired by a team of two

Mirage—French-built fighter-bomber jet operated by Argentine
  Air Force
MO—Medical Officer
MT—Motor Transport
MV—Motor Vessel

NAAFI—Navy, Army and Air Force Institute, an organisation
  that provides canteen and shopping facilities for troops
NCO—Non-commissioned Officer
NGFO—Naval Gunfire Forward Observation Officer, an officer
  of the RA who directs supporting fire from ships during an
  action on land

OC—Officer commanding
Oerlikon—Swedish 20-mm AA cannon, used by Argentines on
  land and on some British ships
'O' Group—Orders Group. A meeting of all a battalion's (or
  other unit's) officers to be briefed by the CO and others
OP—Observation Post, usually a well concealed position forward of a main unit used to report back on enemy dispositions
  and movements

PRI—President of the Regimental Institute
Pucara—Twin piston-engined ground-attack aircraft used by the
  Argentine Air Force

QM—Quartermaster, the battalion officer responsible for supplies and stores

RA—Royal Artillery (properly the Royal Regiment of Artillery)
RAP—Regimental Aid Post, where a battalion's wounded are
  tended and from where, if necessary, they are sent on to
  hospital
Rapier—Ground-to-air missile system comprising a launcher
  mounting four missiles and a tracking system, either visual or
  radar-guided
RCT—Royal Corps of Transport
RE—Royal Engineers (properly the Corps of Royal Engineers)
Recoilless rifle—Anti-tank weapon mainly used by Argentine
  forces in an artillery role

Re-entrant—A valley or ravine running into the side of a hill or slope

Reverse slope—The slope of a hill away from the enemy, that is with the summit between the enemy and troops on a reverse slope

RFA—Royal Fleet Auxiliary

RM—Royal Marines (Corps of Royal Marines)

RMO—Regimental Medical Officer

RSO—Regimental Signals Officer

RSM—Regimental Sergeant-Major

RV—Rendezvous

SA, SAA—Small arms, small-arms ammunition

SAS—Special Air Service Regiment

SBS—Special Boat Squadron. A Royal Marine Commando unit trained in raiding from small craft

Scimitar—Light tank armed with a 30-mm automatic cannon

Scorpion—Light tank armed with a 76-mm gun. Both Scorpion and Scimitar are equipped with precision sighting and night-sighting equipment, and both have excellent cross-country performance

2/IC—Second-in Command

66—66-mm anti-tank rocket, carried by infantry battalions

SLR—Self-loading rifle. Issue 7.62-mm rifle, equipping all British infantry units

Skyhawk (A-4)—American-built jet-powered fighter/bomber, operated by Argentine Air Force

SMG—Submachine-gun

Snowcat—Tracked cross-country vehicle (unarmed) designed for use in snow, but with good performance over rough, soft or wet terrain

SS—Special Service

SS-11—Air-to-air or air-to-ground missile fitted to British light helicopters

Sterling—British issue 9-mm submachine-gun

Stonk—Slang for a mortar bombardment

Sunray—Radio codeword for a commanding officer

Tac HQ—A battalion's tactical HQ, which moves forward with an advance and deals with the battle situation as necessary.

Triple A—20-mm Oerlikon automatic cannon grouped in three on a single mounting

VCP—Vehicle Control Point

WO—Warrant Officer

Zulu time—Greenwich Mean Time, as opposed to local time

Index

Abols, Cpl D., 70, 77n, 167
Adams, Cpl S., 69, 76
Aircraft and helicopters: A-4 Skyhawk, 33, 35, 37, 38, 40, 90, 120, 121, 124, 136, 138; Chinook, 83, 91, 102, 105 and n, 132, 156, 159; C-130 Hercules, 26, 120, 134; Gazelle, 34; Harrier and Sea Harrier, 34, 40, 43, 50–1, 90–1, 123, 124; Huey, 91, 132; Mirage, 33, 37, 40, 120; Pucara, 26, 32, 33, 35, 71, 75, 78, 90, 91, 100, 120; Scout, 104, 105, 151; Sea King, 126
Aird, Sgt I., 63, 73, 168
Ajax Bay, 40, 46, 101, 102, 108, 114, 119, 121
Aldershot, 13, 18, 63, 112
Alexander, Pte S. J., 70, 160
Argentine Air Force: underrated, 44; attacks by, 33, 34, 37, 38, 40, 43, 71, 75, 78, 90, 120, 121–4, 125, 136–7
Argentine army: quality, 11, 26, 27, 44, 45, 62, 65, 120; equipment and rations, 24, 26; dispositions in Falklands, 24, 39, 44; 'surround' beach-head, 34; Darwin/Goose Green dispositions, 49, 54–5; and Darwin/Goose Green battles, 62–4, 65, 67–9, 82–3, 92, 93–4, 95; Darwin Hill surrender, 77, 78–9;

Boca House surrender, 81–2; Goose Green surrender, 96–9; after surrender, 102–3; and possible attack on Fitzroy, 125; on W. Ridge, 133–52; at Stanley, 153–6; casualties, 79, 100, 102, 154; shelling by, 47, 48, 64, 109, 131, 139, 140, 142, 148, 151; treatment of civilians, 99, 154, 156
Army Air Corps, 33, 93, 164, 168–9
Arnold, Maj K., RA, 52, 58, 59–60
Ascension Island, 18, 22, 112, 156

Banks, Cpl, 105, 109
Bardsley, L/Cpl S. A., 167
Barrett, Sgt T. I., 61, 69, 70, 78, 148, 167
Barry, Lt J., 164; Canterra House, 39–40; abortive move south, 42–3; airfield battle, 86; at Schoolhouse, 87, 88; killed, 89, 143
Barton, Cpl, 143, 145
BBC: broadcast before Bn attack, 49–50, 82
Beattie, Sgt J. W., 85
Beaumont, Capt M., 38, 121, 126
Belize, 13, 14
Bell, Capt R., RM, 51, 52, 95, 97
Benest, Capt David, 12
Bentley, L/Cpl M. W. C., 167
Beresford, L/Cpl, 77

Index

Bingley, L/Cpl G. D., 164, 167; killed, 65

Binney, R., 103, 104, 107–8, 125, 126

Bishop, Cpl, 139

Bluff Cove, 123, 156; Argentines in, 104; Bn in, 108–17; civilians in, 111

Boca House, 49, 53, 54, 55, 56, 57, 58, 67, 72, 73, 74, 79, 80, 81, 82, 84, 85

Bone, Pte S., 109

Bonner Bay, 25, 26, 31

Boots, poor quality of, 19–20, 35, 92, 158

Bradford, Cpl, 104

Bramall, F–M Sir E., 113, 178–9

Brigades: 3 Cdo, 38, 39, 168, 169; composition, 16; sails, 16; landing plan, 25; Bn attack, 40–2, 45; Darwin/Goose Green battles, 93, 94, 99, 172–7; move to Stanley, 101, 103, 109, 119; W. Ridge battle, 132, 133, 137, 150; lessons, 160 5 Inf, 15, 101, 105, 126; landing plan, 25; Bn joins, 103; composition, 103 n; at Fitzroy, 108, 111–2, 122–4; move to Stanley, 119–20; battle for Stanley, 133, 151; lessons, 160

British units: Blues and Royals (RHG/D), 97, 126, 129, 132, 158–9, in W. Ridge battles, 133, 135, 138–40, 141–2, 145, 152; Devon and Dorset Regt, 16; 16 Field Ambulance, 121, 122, 123; 1/7th Gurkha Rifles, 101, 103 n, 109, 114, 120, 133, 135; Parachute Regiment, see separate entry; RAF Regt, 20; Royal Anglian Regt, 14, 16; Royal Irish Rangers, 14; 2nd Bn Scots Guards, 103 n, 114–6, 120, 124, 133, 135; SAS, 20, 26, 32, 36, 39, 40, 44, 135, 138, 159; SBS, 26, 30, 31, 114; 1st Bn Welsh Guards, 103 n, 114, 119, 120, 122–5, 133; Welsh Regt, 20

Brooke, Pte A. E., 72, 168

Brookes, Pte L., 70, 148

Buenos Aires, 34

Burntside House, 39, 49, 53, 55, 56, 57, 60, 61, 64, 66, 103; Pond, 60, 61

Butler, Maj, 131

Camilla Creek, 49, 50, 54, 55, 56, 57, 58, 60, 66; House, 40, 42, 45, 46, 48, 49, 51, 58, 60, 61, 75, 78, 83, 84, 93, 96

Camp, Cpl T. J., 67, 69, 167

Canterra House, 39, 40, 42

Carroll, Pte, 149

Carter, Pte G. S., 167

Ceritos Arroyo, 56, 57; House, 40

Challenger, Mt, 109

Chapman, Lt C., 62, 72, 73, 104

Charteris, 74

Chaundler, Lt-Col D., 12; views, 113, 114, 120; joins Bn, 106–7, 108; at Fitzroy/Bluff Cove, 108, 112–4, 116, 117, 125; journey out, 112–3; move from Fitzroy, 125–6; move to Stanley, 130, 132; plans for W. Ridge, 132–9; W. Ridge battle, 141–52; Arg. surrender, 152, 153; service at Darwin, 156

Chile, 22

Clarke, Capt W. J. C., 168

Coe, 2/Lt M., 60, 67, 69–70, 75, 130, 152

Connors, Cpl, 63, 152

Connor, Lt C. S., 46, 49, 51, 60, 84, 106, 107, 167

Constance, Capt D., RM, 17, 117, 126, 149

Cooper, Maj the Rev D., 22, 168; service before landings, 27–8; move to Sussex Mtn, 32; burial of Bn's dead, 100; burial of Arg. dead, 103; at Fitzroy, 122; move to Stanley, 130; service in Stanley, 155; service at Darwin, 156

Caudwell, C/Sgt T., 37

Cork, L/Cpl A., 164; killed 65, 66

Cork, Sgt, RE, 126

Coronation Point, 49, 55, 56, 58, 60

187

Coulson, Capt A., 39, 51, 54–5, 95, 110–11, 120

Creasey, Pte, 139

Crosland, Maj. J., 20, 167; landings, 31; Darwin/Goose Green battles, 62, 63, 67, 80; Boca House, 72, 81; Swan Inlet, 104; at Furze Bush Pass, 131; at W. Ridge, 141

Curtis, Cpl S., 141, 149, 152

Day, Pte, 30

Dance, L/Cpl N. J., 63, 168

Darwin, 24, 25, 26, 36, 39, 49, 52, 103; Args. in, 39; plan for Bn to attack, 40, 43–5, 54–8; description and defences, 52–5; battle for, 59–82, 84; service and memorial at, 156; log of battle, 172–7

Davies, Maj C. M., RE, 108, 112, 168

Dean, Pte, 139

Dent, Capt C., 164; at Darwin Hill, 75, 76; killed, 76

Dey, Pte, 69, 76

Dixon, Pte S. J., 164; killed, 88

Drunken Rock Pass, 136

Dunbar, L/Cpl K. P., 37, 168

Dunkeley, L/Cpl, 142

Ellerby, Capt D. A., 156, 168

Elliott, Cpl, 86, 147

Esplin-Jones, Cdr C. J., 27, 156, 168

Estancia House, 126, 135; Mt, 119, 129

Evans, Cpl A. J., 86, 147

Falklands Islands, *passim*; background to crisis, 13–14; outbreak of war, 22; plan for landings, 24–5, 26; landings, 27–33; Arg. surrender, 154; lessons of campaign, 157–63; media and campaign, 11–12, 26, 36, 49–50, 158

Falkland Sound, 24, 28

Fanford, Ben, 118

Fanning Head, 26

Farrar, Capt P. R., 46, 73, 84, 87, 168

Farrar-Hockley, Maj C. D., 20, 103,

167; at 'O' Group, 54; Darwin/Goose Green battles, 66–7; at Darwin Hill, 69, 70, 71, 74, 75–6, 77; at W. Ridge, 137; advance to Stanley, 152

Fenwick, Sgt-Maj, 71, 153

Ferguson, Pte, 37, 150

Field, Capt R., 126, 129, 132, 142

Fieldhouse, Adm Sir John, 42

Findlay, C/Sgt G. P. M., 164; killed, 140

Fitzroy, 129, 156; plan to move Bn to, 103; Args. in, 103; Bn at, 107–26; Arg. air attack, 121–5

Fletcher, Pte M. W., 164, 168; killed, 66

Forbes, Pte, 73

Fowler, Sgt, 102

Fox Bay, 24

Fox, Robert, 26, 37, 52, 97, 168

Framingham, L/Cpl, 78

French, Pte, 64

Furze Bush Pass, 131, 137

Godfrey, Pte, 88, 89, 139

Godwin, Capt T., 17, 29, 38, 42, 101, 102

Goose Green, 24, 25, 49, 50, 51, 52, 102, 103, 109, 111, 114, 118, 120, 124, 138, 140, 141, 150, 156; SAS raids, 22, 39; Args. in, 39, 47; plan for Bn's attack, 40, 43–5, 54–8; bombardment of, 43; description and defences, 53–5; battle for, 59–100; and BBC broadcast, 82–3; Schoolhouse battle, 84, 85, 86, 87–8, 89, 90; airfield battle, 84–5, 86–7; civilians in, 90, 91, 97, 98, 99, 101; Arg. surrender, 96–9; log of battle, 172–7

Gormley, Pte S. J., 148

Goss, Eric, 94, 99

Government House, 153

Greenhalgh, Capt J. G., RCT, 93, 104, 105, 151, 168

Greenhalgh, Sgt-Maj, 87

Gray, Pte D., 168

Grayling, Pte B. J., 167

Hall, Pte M. W. C., 72
Hannaway, K., 103
Hardcastle, Brooke, 91, 103
Hardman, Cpl D., 69, 70, 164, 168; killed, 76
Harley, Cpl T. W., 146, 167
Harriet, Mt, 103, 108, 109, 119, 122, 127, 151
Hastings, Max, 51
Hastings, Sgt, 70
Hearnden Water, 137
Higginson, Sgt, 47
Hocking, Lt E., 35, 62, 72
Holman-Smith, Pte M. H., 164; killed, 85
Hughes, Capt S. J., RAMC, 37, 46, 47, 78, 84, 102, 114, 122, 130, 168

Illingsworth, Pte S., 72, 164, 167; killed, 73
Island Harbour, 110; House, 110
Iveson, Sqn-Ldr R., 51

Jackson, Lt-Col M., 112
Jenkins, Capt R., 105
Jenner, Maj H., 45; Darwin/Goose Green battles, 56, 59, 66, 74, 85
Jenner, Maj R., 20, 108; Darwin/ Goose Green battles, 73–4, 84–5; wounded, 85; rejoins Bn, 108; and Stanley battles, 129; at W. Ridge, 142
Jones, Lt-Col 'H', 12, 16, 22, 164; prepares for campaign, 14; command set-up, 15; character and qualities, 16; 'O' Group for landings, 24–6, 27; and treatment of POWs, 25–6, 58, 79; and landings, 27, 28, 29, 30; on Sussex Mtn, 34, 35–6; plans for attack, 40, 45–6; and cancellation, 42; and BBC broadcast, 49; at Camilla Creek House, 49–58; Darwin/Goose Green 'O' Group, 52–8; Darwin/ Goose Green battles, 64–5, 66, 67, 74; at Darwin Hill, 75; leads attack, 76–7; wounded, 77; death, 77, 79, 80–1, 92; inspiration and

example, 95, 165–6; VC, 95, 165–6, 167

Keeble, Maj C. P. B., 12, 100, 125, 156, 167; command set-up, 15; character and qualities, 16–17; takes command, 79; Darwin/Goose Green battles, 79–80, 82, 83, 91–2; attempts to gain Arg. surrender, 94–5, 170–1; Arg. surrender at Goose Green, 101, 103; and command of Bn, 106–7; at Fitzroy, 107, 116–7; at W. Ridge, 149
Kennedy, Lt P., 89, 110, 114, 121
Kent, Mt, 42, 103, 105, 109, 119, 126, 127, 129, 130, 132, 133, 136, 137, 138
Ketley, Capt P., 47, 50, 51, 52
Kilmartin, Diana, 111
Kilmartin, Kevin, 111, 116
Kincher, Cpl, 87
Kirkwood, Pte A. T., 70
Knight, Pte, 87, 88, 89

Lafonia, 53, 100'
Lambert, Pte, 150
Light, Sgt, 139
Livingstone, Lt C. R., RE, 52, 56, 126, 169
Longdon, Mt, 119, 127, 130, 131, 132, 135, 136, 137, 142, 149, 169
Lough, Bob, 156
Lower Pass, 139
Mackenzie, WO, RCT, 38
Mansfield, Pte A., 168
Margerison, Cpl M. G., 62, 64, 81
McAuley, Cpl, 145
McCracken, Maj W., RA, 136
McKay, Sgt I., killed, 131; VC, 131, 162, 169
McKee, Pte, 62
McLoughlin, Pte, 150
McNally, Cpl, 36
Mechan, Pte T., 164
Melia, Cpl D., RE, 69, 164; killed, 79
Menendez, Maj-Gen M. B., 97, 153, 154
Meredith, Sgt J. C., 88, 89, 147, 167

Middleton, Capt B., 83
Miller, Maj R., 23, 99n
Miller, Alan, 94
Missiles: Blowpipe, 20, 33, 35, 37, 40, 55, 58, 71, 75, 78, 90, 121; Exocet, 20, 22, 23; Milan, 15, 37, 39, 46, 56, 59, 60, 64, 74, 81, 84, 85, 90, 136, 138; Rapier, 36, 40, 123; Sea Dart, 124; Sidewinder, 90; SS-11, 104, 151
Moody Brook, 133, 135, 138, 145, 146, 147, 151
Moore, Maj-Gen J. J., RM, 103, 113, 133, 155, 168
Morralis, Lt (Arg. POW), 51
Morrell, Pte R. P. G., 168
Morris, C/Sgt A., 104
Mort, Pte P., 65
Morton, Lt-Col P., 112
Murrell Bridge, 130; River, 131, 137, 152

Neame, Maj P., 20, 168; briefed for attack, 40, 45; at Camilla Creek House, 48; Darwin/Goose Green battles, 65, 74, 79–80; Boca House battle, 81; Goose Green battles, 82, 85–6, 87; at W. Ridge, 138, 140, 145, 146, 147, 148, 151
Norman, Sgt, 77
Norris, David, 26, 52, 97, 125, 134
Nunn, Capt R. J., RM, 164, 169; killed, 78

O'Rourke, Pte E., 78, 168
Osborne, Maj M., 136
Owen, Cpl, 85, 148, 150, 153

Page, Lt J. D., 143, 147, 168
Pain, Pte, 69
Parachute Regiment: 1st Bn, 20; 2nd Bn—*see* 2 Para; 3rd Bn (3 Para), 16, 35, 59, 116, 127, 129–30, 156; Mt Longdon battle, 130, 131, 169; VC, 131, 162, 169; awards, 169; message from CGS, 179
Parr, Pte D. A., 65, 164; killed, 145

Peatfield, Sgt-Maj, 85
Pebble Island, 24, 26
Pedroza, Air Vice-Cdre Wilson Dosio, 97, 98
Penman, Sqn-Ldr J., 47, 50
Philpott, Pte, 63, 141, 149
Pike, Lt-Col H., 136, 156
Pioggi, Lt-Col I., 97
Poole, Pte, 72
Port Sussex House, 40; Inlet, 47
Prior, Cpl S. R., 164; killed, 70
Pye, Sgt, 83

Rees, Pte, 70
Rice, Maj A., RA, 45–6, 83, 97
Royal Artillery: support for Bn, 46, 52, 55, 56, 57, 138, 150, 145, 151; 8 Bty, 29 Cdo Regt, 55, 83, 91; 29 Fd Bty, 108; 47th AD Regt, 55–6
Royal Corps of Transport, 38, 83, 168
Royal Engineers, 100, 102, 133, 146, 164, 168, 169; 9 Para Sqn, 108, 112, 126, 150; 59 Ind Cdo Sqn, 52, 126, 150; in Darwin/Goose Green battles, 52
Royal Marines, 56, 58, 90, 168, 169; 40 Cdo, 16, 26, 133; 42 Cdo, 16, 96, 127, 133; 45 Cdo, 16, 59, 127, 129
Russell, Pte S., 70, 85
Ryan, Maj M., 20, 58, 113, 118

Salinas Beach, 40
San Carlos, 25, 44, 45, 55, 59, 83, 94, 101, 103; Water, 24, 37, 100, 101, 120
Sapper Hill, 120, 136
Schoolhouse (Goose Green), 55, 82, 84, 85, 86, 87, 88, 89, 90
Shaw, Lt J., 61
Shaw, Cpl, 97
Ships: *Ambuscade*, support at W. Ridge, 138, 145, *Antelope*, sunk, 34, 43, *Antrim*, 34, *Ardent*, sunk, 34, 37, *Arrow*, support at Darwin/Goose Green, 45, 55, 57, 60, 65, 71, 72, *Atlantic Conveyor*, 20–2, (sunk) 43, 159, *Belgrano*,

Index

sunk, 22, *Brilliant*, 33, *Broadsword*, 27, 43, *Canberra*, 16, 17, 34, *Coventry*, sunk, 43, *Europic*, 17, 156, 168, *Fearless*, 38, *Intrepid*, 28, 29, 39, 114, *Monsunen*, 119, *Norland*, 33, 34, 39, 47, 121, 155, 168; converted, 17; sails, 17; voyage, 18–27; air defence, 20, 38; landings, 27–31; offloading Bn's stores, 33, 37–8, 43; brings 1/7th Gurkhas, 101; takes 2 Para home, 156, *Plymouth*, 124, *Sheffield*, sunk, 22, *Sir Galahad*, bombed in San Carlos Water, 38; arrives at Fitzroy, 121; bombed at Fitzroy, 122–4, *Sir Launcelot*, 38, 155, *Sir Tristram*, 121; bombed, 122, *Uganda*, 93

Simpson, RSM, 22–3, 32, 33, 36 100, 117; Darwin/Goose Green battles, 71; Arg. surrender at Goose Green, 99; at Fitzroy, 122

Slough, Pte P., 164; killed, 146

Smith, Sgt-Maj, 56

Smith, L/Cpt N. R., 164; killed, 89

South Georgia, 13, 22, 43, 101

Spencer, Cpl, 67

Spencer, Sgt, 84

Stadden, Cpl, 86

Stanley, 24, 25, 26, 96; airfield bombed, 22; bombardment, 43; plans to attack, 119–20, 127; battles for, 133–52; Arg. surrender, 153, 154–6

Steele, Pte G. A., 149

Sullivan, Cpl P. S., 86, 88, 164; killed, 89

Sussex Mtn, 25, 26, 31, 32, 33, 34, 36, 37, 39, 40, 42, 46, 47, 48, 51, 52, 59, 61, 83, 92, 94, 114

Swan Inlet, 104; House, 104

Teal Inlet, 126

Thatcher, Rt Hon M., MP, 14, 27, 30

Thayer, L/Cpl, 83

Thomas, Pte, 85

Thompson, Brig J. H., RM, 45, 156, 168; Darwin/Goose Green battles,

45, 94; move to Stanley, 130; battle for Stanley, 133; Arg. surrender, 152

Thurman, Lt J., 52, 53, 54

Tighe, L/Cpl L. A., 88

Tuffen, Pte S. M., 69

Tumbledown, Mt, 120, 133, 135, 138, 143, 148, 151

Tunn, Pte J. A., 85

2 Para (2nd Bn, The Parachute Regt), *passim*; in Second World War and other theatres, 12, 162; before Falklands campaign, 13, 14; warned for Falklands, 14; equipment and composition, 14–15; joins 3 Cdo Bde, 16; sails, 17; training on *Norland*, 18–19; at Ascension, 22, 179; plans for landing, 25–6; landings, 28–31; on Sussex Mtn, 31–46; abortive move south, 40–2; plans to attack Darwin/Goose Green, 40, 43–5, 46, 55–8; move to Camilla Creek House, 46–8; at Camilla Creek House, 48–60; and BBC broadcast, 49–50; first POWs, 51; Darwin/Goose Green battles, 59–100; 1st objectives taken, 61–4, 65–6; Darwin Hill battle, 67–79; Boca House battle, 72–4, 79–82; and CO's death, 77, 78, 80–1, 92; attacks and invests Goose Green, 82–3, 84, 93; Schoolhouse battle, 84, 85, 86, 87–8, 89; airfield battle, 84–5, 86–7; Arg. surrender at Goose Green, 96–9; burial of dead, 100; in Goose Green, 101–5; plan for Fitzroy move, 103; joins 5 Inf Bde, 103; Swan Inlet raid, 104; move to Fitzroy/Bluff Cove, 105–9; at Fitzroy/Bluff Cove, 107–26; captures Arg. OP, 110–1; voyage back to Fitzroy, 117–8; air attack on Fitzroy, 121–3; rejoins 3 Cdo Bde, 125, 126, 127; move to Furze Bush Pass, 127–32; plan for Stanley attack, 127; W. Ridge battles, 132–52; 1st objectives taken, 142; main ridge battle, 143–51; 1st Br.

troops in Stanley, 152–3; meeting with Gen. Menendez, 153; in Stanley, 154–6; service in Stanley, 155; service at Darwin, 156; return, 156; awards, 161–2, 167–9; Roll of Honour, 164; message from CGS, 113, 178–9; casualties, 79, 100, 154; lessons, 34–5, 157–63; qualities, 12, 162–3
Two Sisters, 119, 127, 130, 135

Usborne, Mt, 104

Waddington, 2/Lt C., 47–8, 81, 139, 150–1
Wagon, Capt R., RAMC, 46, 84, 102, 123
Walker, L/Cpt, 151
Wallis, 2/Lt G., 46, 60, 61, 67, 71, 84, 168

Warden, Pte, 70
Watson, Pte, 70
Webster, Lt S., 48, 65, 86, 87, 139, 147, 153
Weighell, Lt G. R. 62, 63, 72, 168
William, Mt, 120, 133
Wilson, Brig A., 103, 104, 105, 113, 116, 122, 133
Williamson, Pte, 73
Wireless Ridge: plans to attack, 132, 133–9; description and defences, 132–3; battle for, 139–52
Wood, Capt D. A., 23, 36, 66, 164; at Darwin Hill, 75–6; killed, 76, 79
Woodward, Rear-Adm J. F., 42, 113
Worsley-Tonks, A/Capt M. S. H., 164
Wreck Point, 29

Young, Capt J., 73